Keys to Freedom

How to Unlock
Your Ability to
Thrive in Changing Times.

Robyn Hodge

A catalogue record for this book is available from the National Library of New Zealand.

ISBN 978 0 473 44322 1 (paperback). ISBN 978 0 473 44323 8 (eBook). ISBN 978 0 473 44324 5 (audiobook).

This Book: Paperback, eBook and Audiobook – are all written and spoken in New Zealand (British) English. At times specific American or other spellings are used such as in the references in the Resource section.

Keys to Freedom
How to Unlock Your Ability to Thrive in Changing Times.

The Book:

"A soothing balm for your inner critic."
"Empowering, uplifting and inspiring."

Robyn Hodge

The Coach:

"So insightful and encouraging."
"I come away feeling enthused and inspired."

TABLE OF CONTENTS

DEDICATION

This is in dedication to you all. Thank you for being in my life.

Thank you to my precious family, past, present and future, including those who are no longer with us in physical form, but are unbounded and omnipresent.

Eternal thanks for the deep love my mum shares and a special dedication to my dad, who passed away during the writing of the first version of this book.

To my husband and children, I love you so much. To our children: You inspire me with your love, courage and humour as you step into the lives you love regardless of external pressures.

To my friends: I am grateful for your friendship and willingness to have fun with me and explore new possibilities too.

For those of you I don't yet know, nor ever met, I thank you, because you too have called this book forth and your desire has cumulated in me writing this to enhance the lives of many.

May you find your love, power, joy and wisdom, that is ready and waiting for you. Let it now come clear. Allow the ties of the past to untangle and be released. May our attempts to explain the interconnectedness of everything have us embracing unity in our diversity. Receive the goodness of the new amazing now. To all the realms, all the galaxies, the unified field of intelligence, or however you call the infinity of space, I thank you for heralding us in.

Written, spoken and infused with love, light and infinite gratitude.

ACKNOWLEDGEMENTS

 I am so grateful of the melting pot of inspiration throughout time available from many sources. I read, listened, watched, travelled, questioned and learnt so much from everybody.

In some places I will quote people and their work. If your name doesn't get seen on these pages, with credit for something, please receive this in my collective thanks and appreciation. You matter and your reading and listening to this now makes a beautiful difference too.

I am so grateful for my husband reading all my very long first draft and then reading this next shortened version as well. Not only did he check my work and provide great feedback and suggestions he used the tools and reminders in this book also. He was already awesome and went to another level of awesomeness.

The enthusiasm and interest when I shared snippets of my book was heartwarming and inspiring, especially as I got closer to the finished product. Thank you to all my beautiful family and friends, clients and colleagues, old and new! May you be smiling and excited now that it's here and you finally get to enjoy it all. Audrey and Monique deserve a special mention, I am so grateful for your keen interest and feedback.

I must add Ged Cusack in, he resisted at first and then came on board to help me with further editing of my first version, taking it to the next level. Thank you so much. Ged has now written 6 non-fiction and 2 fiction books. As for the cover I am so grateful for Christchurch Visual Brander, Craig Burton. He worked his magic in 2018 and 7 years later I felt called to do some extra fine tuning and he created this purple version as well.

May this book be so special for you. Soothing to the soul and Inspiring to your heart, mind and body.

INTRODUCTION

Do you sometimes feel stuck, as if you are living through the film "Groundhog Day," or continually banging your head against the same wall?

Are you constantly experiencing roadblocks that hold you in survival mode and stop you from thriving?

If you are facing any sort of disruption or pressure in your life, then this book is for you.

There are keys here that can fit the locks and remove the blocks. A transformational journey is here for you. Consider this a recipe book for living your best life now. This is a book filled with tips, tools and techniques, so you may thrive.

Remember you are not alone, and the good news is that you can change your situation.

There is another level of your amazing life for you to experience.

This level is a place with more joy, abundance, inspiration and fulfilment.

Let's uncover more of this, so you may continue to grow and evolve and experience far more happiness than ever before. This time with the keys and without the pressure that was felt before.

In this book you are about to experience that growth!

Having spent much of my life on a journey of personal development, I have condensed some important learning's for you, from ancient wisdom to modern scientific research. I've also provided you the insights and understandings that many of the greatest leaders, philosophers, and educators have used to excel in their own lives.

Even if you don't quite feel this yet, remember that it is all okay. You are in the right place at the right time.

HOW TO USE THIS BOOK

This book is peppered with questions for you. You'll have answers and solutions to explore.

I've provided exercises in each chapter to play with too, so that you can determine personal solutions tailored just for you.

Treat this as being written to and for you. Let the words come to life and use them to break through and dissolve the roadblocks of anything that has troubled you in the past.

Having a journal beside you to write in is beneficial as well. Call it your "Keys to Freedom Journal."

It is time for you to step forward into the best you, you can now be.

There Is More for You to Hear and See

Some of you reading this are opening, maybe for the first time. Some of you have opened up before, got hurt, things didn't seem to work, and then you closed up again.

Others of you are seasoned travellers and recognise this ground, but this time it's different and there are even more gifts for you to receive.

My hope is this book becomes a "go to" book for you - for whenever life strikes a chord for a new vibration.

• Enjoy the gems in here for you to uncover and discover.

• Enjoy many readings, checking back to specific chapters, highlighting and bookmarking.

• Enjoy finding a new or deeper level of understanding in every reading.

• Enjoy asking a question and open a page for your answers.

• Enjoy using it to serve you well.

Know that there will be answers for you here. Are you willing to face your resistance and let more goodness in?

Let the unfolding begin for your highest good. Here it is, come and get it. A journey for you, that appeals to your deep knowing, heart's desires and wisdom within.

CHAPTER 1: IT'S NEVER TOO LATE

"It is never too late to be what you might have been." George Eliot

If you have a curious mind like I do, you might be interested to know that the author of that quote, "George," was the pen name of English Novelist Mary Ann Evans (1819–1880). She was also a poet, journalist, translator, and one of the leading writers of the Victorian era. Everything may not be as it seems, or as we think it is.

She is often heralded as the literary force behind one of Britain's greatest ever novels, *Middlemarch.* But for much of her life, and even today, she is better known by her male pseudonym, George Eliot, which she adopted to conceal her gender at a time when women were excluded from intellectual circles. "Throughout history, many female writers have used male pen names for their work to be published or taken seriously."

Evans' secret identity became a source of widespread speculation in Victorian England after several of her stories, published under the George Eliot pen name, gained popularity. Charles Dickens, author of *Great Expectations, A Christmas Carol* and *Oliver Twist,* even wrote her a letter expressing his admiration and curiosity.

Evans longed to write back and come clean, lamenting to her publisher that "the iron mask of my incognito seems quite painful" in light of Dickens' praise. The following year, people began misattributing her work to various individuals and the secret began leaking from her inner circle, leading the author to reluctantly reveal her identity.

In 2020 the project "Reclaim her name" had books republished under the female authors real names. Her famous novel was one of them.

Living Your Dreams

It doesn't matter the perceptions of others, your race, gender, or age; it's never too late to start living your dreams now. You may not achieve all that you would wish, but you can have fun seeing how far you can get.

Charles Darwin, English naturalist, geologist, and biologist, widely known for his contributions to evolutionary biology didn't publish his breakthrough book *On the Origin of Species* until 1859 at aged 50. This transformed the way we understand the natural world with ideas that, in his day, were nothing short of revolutionary.

Judi Dench, Dame Judith Olivia Dench is an English actress. Widely considered one of Britain's greatest actors, she is noted for her versatility, having appeared in films and television programmes. She was in her 60's when her film career took off and is still starring in movies in her 80's.

Yuichiro Miura, Japanese skier and alpinist became the oldest person to reach the top of Mount Everest in 2014 at age 80 and said he would like to try again at age 90.

WW11 veteran, South African Mohr Keet, became the world's oldest bungee jumper in 2010 at the age of 96. He didn't begin jumping until the age of 88.

And at age 92, Gladys Burrill entered the *Guinness Book of World Records* as the oldest female to compete in a marathon. Her fifth Honolulu finish in seven years, Burrill's race time was nine hours, 53 minutes, and 16 seconds.

If you're 25, you don't have to wait, you can live your best life now.

Your Genius

With all this in mind, let's tap into more of our own genius story. The original basis of this book was the paradigm of life unfolding in paradise. Paradise is being able to experience bliss, joy and delight even if you are not surrounded by natural beauty and even if you feel the world is in a state of flux and crisis.

I acknowledge the anxiety, uncertainty and concern people feel. There is also the new story based in love, hope and inspiring actions to unfold, waiting to be told.

I wrote a lot, and ¾ of the way through, I was asked to write a book about growth without pressure. How do we do this? I felt honoured to be asked, and excited because I had already written so much. Knowing that what I had to say was valued and that there were many more who wanted to hear and read what I had to share was a privilege I respected.

This first chapter is like opening a suitcase and seeing it full of gifts. We will get a glimpse of many and unpack them the best we can in these coming chapters.

Pressure

It's very difficult to achieve the conditions needed to turn coal into diamonds. Diamonds are made of pure carbon compressed under extreme pressure and heat.

Growth

Without exposure to adversity or pressure, our resilience doesn't have an opportunity to develop; too much, however, will overwhelm us, having a negative impact. It was all about finding that sweet spot.

Growth Without Pressure

So, for a while, *Growth Without Pressure* was the title. Then I recalled that it's never too late in many situations and there was another step beyond this. That step is unlocking the genius in us, finding and using the keys within, so we create the best lives we can. Finding out how we can thrive, regardless of the changing times. Often, we lock ourselves in a cage with limiting beliefs and much evidence to validate it. We take on these limits as truths and find they are perspectives that have blocked our way.

Breaking through old paradigms and stories, thriving in changing times, having our own unique keys. Attaining empowerment, feeling liberated and enjoying freedom. Sunlight, water, air, shelter, good food and clothing. Someone to love. Something to do. Something to look forward to.

In reviewing what people wanted, a healthy mind, body and relationships were key. Improving our talents in the world so we may prosper together.

The beauty of all this is that it merges into the oneness of life itself. As your life unfolds here on your version of paradise, you get to grow and evolve and your keys to freedom await you. It's never too late to appreciate what has been and what else can be.

Spinning Plates

Imagine you have two spinning plates, if you put all your focus on one, the other may fall and break. This is a bit like life, get good at what you're doing now and look forward in awareness, because if you don't, like the plates, you may spin out. Instead of feeling like you're making breakthroughs you may find it feels like you're breaking down, crashing and burning.

• You are already amazing, even if you don't know, or feel this "yet."

• Come to this space and look again to discover more gems that are here for you and within you too.

• Keys to thrive, love and enjoy it all, without the pressure and restraint you had before.

In Your Power

Each morning: "I accept, I thank, I surrender."

Each night, a clearing exercise such as:

"I release."

"I release everything that is not for my highest good, growth and joy. Thank you."

"I release everything mentally, physically, emotionally, nutritionally and spiritually that is not for my highest good, growth and joy. Thank you."

And I call in:

"I call in, and allow in, with ease and grace, all that is for my highest good, growth and joy. Thank you."

"I trust all is working out well and all is well. Thank you."

Utilising Louise Hay's "All is well" mantra is a great tool to use here also.

"All is well. Everything is working out for my highest good. Out of this situation only good will come. I am safe."

Louise was an American motivational author, professional speaker and AIDS advocate and founded Hay House Publishing.

Intentional Living

This means by implementing such tools, you are being intentional in your life. Being intentional can lead to better decisions that align with your values, can improve your emotional and mental health, can help you enjoy your daily life more, and lead to increased productivity.

You are setting the day up to be in your power. What you used to see as frustrations can now turn into your fuel. What if you were to believe that life really is happening for your highest good and growth? How can you now use these situations more powerfully? You can choose to move to a higher light and a better vantage point.

As you're reading, or listening to this book, or choosing the recommended experience of doing both, notice that there may be a strong stirring within you. This stirring is to be more, perhaps to even do more, but a yearning to enjoy the life you are blessed to have so much more. Consider this question for yourself.

• "What could be an even better way forward for me?"

Intentions: To also be Open, Flexible, Adaptable, and Resourceful.

Did you know that the latest research suggests you have influence of over 95% of your well-being? Another interesting statistic is 75-90% of our diseases have their origins in stress.

Your body is cosmic. Our brain structures have corresponding cosmic counterparts, the sun, moon, planets and stars, directly influencing our mind, body, behaviour. The connection between human physiology and the cosmos is evident in the daily and monthly cycles that pervade the human body. Our bodies are the coolest things we will own. There is genius in nature and genius in our own bodies.

As the quote from Rumi the 13th-century poet said:

"You are not a drop in the ocean. You are the ocean in a drop."

Leonard Cohen, Canadian songwriter, singer, poet, and novelist said;

"If you don't become the ocean, you'll be seasick every day."

Be intentional and be the amazing you. Let's start with having that open mind and an open heart. No surgery is required, see this as a kind and loving heart, and a willingness to thrive. We can address any chronic illnesses and challenges you've faced by knowing many things that were once considered woo-woo have now been proven in science. The realisation of epigenetics (beyond your genes) and more good news is becoming available. Keep exploring and evolving.

Thank you for being here now, you are part of the group helping lead the way of discovery.

Receive this knowledge and use it to realise there is so much more here for you too.

Expectations

Have these tripped you up?

• Expectations not met, so disappointment and frustration set in. You've been told that's an easy fix, simply lower your expectations and you'll feel much better. That's a bit of fun to think, but long term is that the real answer, or could you be selling yourself short?

This is when you might feel the "should" syndrome trying to attack you. Your inner critic is trying to protect you. Thanks for the help, but this is time for your inner coach to show up. What is your inner coach suggesting? It's perhaps time for making a new choice.

Mindset

• If you've been spending more time worrying about how tough it's been and accidentally bringing this to the table now, let's package these feelings up and transform them. May that sound and feel more freeing, transmuting those worries. Allow all your experiences and expectations to take you to another level of your best life.

• No pressure, just relief, gratitude and yes, I'm ready.

As you adjust this could still mean you might appear to be falling 7 times, just get up 8 times.

• Are you ready to feel more relief now?

Excitement

Don't put off your excitement because you're afraid you'll be disappointed, enjoy the excitement. The key is not to hold on too tightly and get attached to how it must be. If it doesn't work out, be mindful that you can still choose to get excited again for the next thing. It's a bit like the line from Tennyson, "Tis better to have loved and lost than never to have loved at all." Lord Alfred Tennyson wrote that after his closest friend died suddenly in 1833 at the age of 22.

Let's look at life through the eyes of love.

Some years ago, we arranged a family holiday to Europe. This created a great deal of excitement, something we felt we would all love. We were looking forward to the adventure. Unfortunately, it had to be cancelled due to issues with the airline. Rather than choosing to feel sad and deflated at missing out on the trip I focussed on the 6 months of enjoyment I had experienced. I had been quite mindful during the process, not striving to be positive, nor pushing any negative thoughts away. Even though this didn't go ahead, I was still happy and able to reflect on the planning and anticipation of this travel. I could remind myself how fascinating and exciting all the places and possibilities were and still are.

Go all in on life, embrace it, be discerning rather than tentatively tiptoeing through. No longer letting fears hold you back as much. Some of our fears are innate, like the fear of falling, loud noises, predators, heights and rapidly approaching objects, while others are learned through experience. Learned fears are like the fear of failure, rejection, uncertainty, loneliness, death, the unknown, not being good enough, poverty, ill health, judgement and criticism. These may sound or feel all too familiar. There are many great resources as well as more tips throughout this book of how to handle such fears more effectively too.

Your Next Step

Set the intention to allow yourself to open to more light and more love in your world. Don't oppose the darkness, bring the light. It's not too late to do this shift.

There are so many ways of being and well-meaning people putting pressure on you to conform to their way of doing things. The question for you to ask yourself:

• Am I remembering the magic ingredient of me, my gifts and unique ways?

This isn't in a self-centred way, but honouring yourself, keeping your own cup full and overflowing, so you have more to give and receive.

You listen and learn and get overwhelmed at times, things aren't working for you that seem to work for others. You are feeling on the outer, a bit different, not quite connected, but pretend it's all okay. There's something missing, but you don't quite know what it is. What can you do just a little differently that can have a positive outcome and result?

Questions

• Am I trying too hard to fit in?

• How can I find a balance here to honour myself a little more?

• Or where can I give a little, if I've become too rigid?

Keep in mind the way you are operating is either enabling or impeding your growth. Sometimes people find they are only accepted if they act a particular way. I like to call this the purple streak.

The Tale of the Purple Streak

Imagine yourself getting a purple streak in your hair. Suddenly you are not taken as seriously, your work is still at a high level, but those around you are uncomfortable and you're finding it harder to fit in. It was just a dare you had, and you're determined to see it out. You're still delivering high quality output, but all the talk is how you look even though this is not having a detrimental effect on your actual work. In fact, your output has increased, and profits are good. You realise you were only accepted before because you conformed. Your unique expression is not valued, you come to the realisation that the environment you thrive in is one allowing full expression and that is not here. The hair colour fades, but how they judged you doesn't. You go elsewhere.

This is a story that happened. It was quite a shock for the team that she resigned, but it was about her being true to herself which is way beyond the purple streak in her hair.

There's a new Earth in the form of a new world opening for all of us. This can be created from tapping into our innate wisdom. Various spiritual and religious groups see this as creating Heaven on Earth. Many in the Scientific community see this as being created from the Unified Field. This is a field of nothing, but the scientists say that out of this nothing emerges everything that is a thing. Ancient Vedic science, the Science of Consciousness, has always known this field. This Unified Field, ocean of consciousness, is said to have qualities, a field of unbounded intelligence, unbounded creativity, unbounded happiness, unbounded love, energy and peace. A place we can tap into.

As you have probably already noticed, some of the old ways are simply not working on our planet, causing it harm and not serving you, me or humanity. We are the caretakers, stewards of the Earth, responsible for preserving the environment and using natural resources wisely.

Maybe you're not willing to stay small, but instead step into your personal power, your unboundedness.

A Quiet Revolution is Occurring

Evolution or revolution? Notice your ability to step out of your comfort zone and current perceptions. Come play and explore a little more.

For more ease and joy in your life, whether it is in health, relationships, work, finances, love, your spiritual world, or all the above remember:

• "You are Strong. You Are Capable and You Are Loved."

• "Life Is Happening **for** You and Not to You."

This means it's time to not be so hard on yourself, or others. Our society has tried to hardwire these judgements and beliefs into us, which in some ways have been helpful to keep us safe, but you are beyond these confines now.

See yourself releasing the belief, or need of things being too hard, or difficult. What have been your previous quick fixes? Notice and see if processed foods, alcohol, or other drugs of your choice were your default. Instead, you may choose to unlock your ability to say goodbye to the need for such short-lived external highs. Make the shift to being high on life itself.

May you have sustained feelings of peace, bliss and ease, as you flow with the rhythm of life. Living in harmony with your needs, desires and talents met.

Life Unfolding

 Many of us are online in our technologically advanced societies. I used to spend time on social media carefully choosing quotes and matching these with photographs we'd taken on our travels and then posting them. The purpose was to enhance and inspire with love and playfulness.

Was this quote an original quote from me? "Maybe not." Was it an original from the other person? Often, the answer was, "Maybe not." Just like there are no original paintings, as they are first drawn in the mind, that too can be said of the written word. Varying sources from varying times in history attributed their name to it. Maybe it's all inspiration that the universe is sending to and through us all to share and enjoy? You are a conduit of this wisdom too.

A lot of people follow the work of Napoleon Hill, and many books were inspired by his book, *Think and Grow Rich.* Published in 1937, - it is among the top 10 best-selling self-help books of all time.

Oliver Napoleon Hill (1883 - 1970) was born into poverty in rural Virginia in the late 19th century and became a member of the Motivational Speakers Hall of Fame. Two of his famous quotes were:

"The man who does more than he is paid for will soon be paid for more than he does."

" A quitter never wins-and-a winner never quits."

Many used Napoleon's inspired thought within their books and video courses. One such person was Canadian Bob Proctor (1934-2022), a new thought self-help author and business owner who created the book and video course You Were Born Rich in 1984. Proctor went from being a child with a poor self-image and little ambition until the early 1960's when the book *Think and Grow Rich,* was shared with him. He claimed his life started to change as the book shifted his focus in life. His first enterprise was a company offering cleaning services, this venture netted him over $100,000 in his starting year despite having neither formal education nor business training. He went on to have an international reputation for getting the very best out of both people and businesses.

An interesting note is that the book, *Think and Grow Rich,* was mostly penned by Napoleon's second wife Rosa Lee Hill (nee Beeland) and not him.

The questions you may reflect upon: "Are you well known as Napoleon Hill?" "Are you doing beautiful, seemingly invisible great work like Rosa Lee Hill?" "Or is there something else you wish to do, create and explore?"

Optimism and Resilience

Find which way forward feels good for you. See how you can tap into more of your gifts. May you be a conduit of even more wisdom. Utilise optimism and resilience in the face of setbacks. If you are breathing, it is not too late for you to bravely pursue what speaks to your heart. You might encounter people that tell you it's too late. You might have reminders in your day of times you've failed. Amidst all the uncertainty you can still hope. Use hope to strengthen you. Even if you do not achieve all you desire, it's going to work out in the end.

"Everything works out in the end; if it hasn't worked out, it's not the end."

Tracy McMillan: American Author and Television Writer. A recurring line by the character Sonny in The Best Exotic Marigold Hotel 2011. So regardless of where you are at, if something didn't go as planned or things seem like a disappointment, and it didn't succeed you can still have fun with this. There's always the potential for something positive to happen in the future. It doesn't mean there are no more opportunities or positive outcomes ahead.

With joy you have the ability to tap into more of your life of miracles.

Let it all be, no pressure.

"Let it be," was also a number one hit song by the Beatles. Ironically it was released in 1970, a month after the group's break-up. "Speaking words of wisdom; let it be." It also won an Academy Award for Best Original Song Score for the 1970 documentary film Let It Be.

Another beautiful reminder from the lyrics of this song: "When the night is cloudy there is still a light that shines on me."

May you feel the freedom without the pressure to conform to certain ideals and step into your light and make more of the amazing you.

Remember that it's all okay. You're in the right place at the right time.

CHAPTER 2: IMAGINE

"Whether you think you can, or think you can't, you're right." Henry Ford

Henry Ford (1863-1947) was born to Irish Immigrant parents and grew up on a farm in Michigan. As an American businessman, inventor and innovator he was famous for creating the Model T, the first mass-produced car. He also introduced the moving assembly line to car production, and invented and popularised the 5-day 40-hour work week. His work made cars more affordable and accessible to the middle class and changed the way people lived.

Imagine

Do you think you can too? A new path is opening for you to explore. Perhaps there is something else that you have not yet done or thought of before.

Visualise yourself walking down a valley, smelling the freshness as you look across the lush green fields. The strong tall trees are whispering to you in the breeze. Your feet crunch on the leaves. You notice a stream off to your right. The water is sparkling as it flows by. A golden light catches your eye, and the warmth of the sun is tickling your cheeks. Some butterflies are fluttering by twinkling in the air. Birds are singing sweetly, and you are experiencing more joy, clarity and oneness with all - and so it is.

If you are still looking for the path to walk down, a valley, or place that you love let's start here.

Let go of what your current capabilities and achievements are and ask yourself, "What would I do if I had all the skill in the world?" Allow a high emotional connection. This art of feeling and saying your desire, or vision out loud and the art of writing it down have a creative power not to be underestimated. Take action, perhaps working toward this vision for 30 minutes a day. Open yourself up to more of your greatness, willingness and availability to step into your greatest potential. Winning sports teams do this successfully, and perhaps you have already done this too. How about taking it to another level of possibility, you are worthy.

Let's have a play with this now:

• State your name, while standing in gratitude and perhaps even with a sense of relief. Already knowing that your true desires are in existence in your life.

• Verbalise your desire/desires out loud and in written form. Do this with strong intent and conviction that these desire/desires are yours.

That is a great first step.

If your enquiring mind wants a study, or some evidence outside of your own experience, or to encourage you to act, here is one for you. Back in 1979 a Harvard study was performed and followed up 10 years later in 1989. What they found was that 3% of Harvard MBAs were earning, on average, ten times as much as the other 97% combined.

Of this study group:

• 84% had no specific goals at all.

• 13% had goals, but they were not committed to paper.

• The 13% of the class who had goals were earning, on average, twice as much as the 84 percent who had no goals at all.

• And as for the 3% - they had clear, written goals and plans to accomplish them.

Given the evidence above we can see that this is a powerful concept. Let's explore some positive possibilities, however you choose to attempt this. It could be by dipping your feet in, diving in, or jumping in with a great splash. Even in shallow water one gets wet, so whichever way you choose, with no harm to yourself or others is great. Keep moving forward, gathering and practicing skills. One day you may find yourself with abilities you never dreamed of. May you be fully immersed in the joys of life, gliding through the water, swimming freely with more ease and effortlessness.

If you're already seasoned with this concept, let's fine tune it a little and feel the excitement of what you currently call miracles, becoming mainstream and a normal part of your life.

Vibrations

Sounds are vibrations that travel through solids, liquids and gasses. Everything in existence, including humans, emits a unique energetic wave or vibration, which can be influenced by our thoughts, emotions, and actions.

Your thoughts are vibrating out:

• What you think can be what you get.

• If you state negative, negative can show up in your life.

• Check in with your inner talk regularly.

When someone gives you a compliment what does your inner chat say instantly? Do you outwardly say, "thank you" or "no I'm not - no I don't" and what about inwardly? Do you know you deserve the compliment, or are you inwardly denying any ownership of that quality/action etc?

Affirmations

Sending out a strong intention, as if you are that already... "I am." Through the universe; - *insert your name here, "(I.......)* have brought in the support of light, love, wisdom and I am enjoying the wonderful miracles that are unfolding in all areas of my life. Each and every day I am improving in each and every way."

"If it's to be, it's up to me."

Please be the change you do want to see.

What if that doesn't do it for you? Is your default currently one of negative thoughts first?

Negativity Bias

Imagine a day in which five good things happen to you, but then you step in a puddle and ruin your shoes. If you were to consider your day ruined – negativity bias – this would be an example of negativity dominance.

By making pessimistic assumptions about how another person will react, we can also fall into the trap of letting our (unwarranted) attitudes impact our behaviours.

By focusing or over-emphasising the potential negatives of a decision, research shows that we become more inclined to avoid risk. (Kahneman & Tversky, 2013).

When facing a choice with potential benefits and risks, therefore, we tend to consider the latter more – an example of negative potency in action (Rozin & Royzman, 2001).

From an organisational perspective, we can look at Kodak, once one of the world's leading photographic film companies. By choosing to remain focused on its core 'strength' (photographic film) and not explore the growing digital photography trend, it lost its competitive position to rivals Sony, Canon, and Fujifilm before filing for bankruptcy in 2002 (Wilson, n.d.).

Research suggests that we can start to tackle negativity bias in the workplace by upping the ratio of positive to negative comments that we give. (Zenger & Folkman, 2013).

To boost team performance and lead others more effectively, in other words, a good ratio to aim for is 5:1. Try it.

Early humans' tendency to focus more on negative thoughts and potential threats is considered a "negativity bias. " This cognitive bias states that negative information has a greater impact on our psychological state than positive information and is believed to have evolved as a survival mechanism for our ancestors.

Survival Advantage

In a dangerous environment, being more attentive to potential threats (like predators or hostile situations) would significantly increase the chances of survival, even if it meant sometimes overreacting to perceived dangers.

Our brains are wired to prioritise negative stimuli, meaning we tend to remember negative experiences more vividly than positive ones.

Implications

While negativity bias was adaptive in our evolutionary past, it can sometimes lead to negative consequences in modern life, like increased anxiety, pessimism, and dwelling on negative thoughts.

So, try upping your ratio of positive to negative comments.

Step into your attitude of gratitude and every perceived negative that comes up, you can now also turn it around and into an afformation.

Afformations

These are about what you do want, and asking a question that assumes what you want is already true. When creating these for yourself start them off with "why am I," "why am I so good at…?" This gets you asking better questions and changes what your brain focuses on. Your brain is searching for why and your job is to take new actions based on your new assumptions. Here are some examples you can use:

• "I can't do this" could be changed to, "why am I so good at doing this?"

• "I don't feel supported and appreciated" could be changed to, "why am I receiving so much support and appreciation?"

Thank you so much for accepting this challenge and stepping up and into more of your greatness and wisdom. What you may have once considered "flaky" and "can't possibly work," is instead a rather powerful tool.

Challenges

As you walk this path and accept these challenges there are some other statements you may like to use. I've found these ones very helpful, and I use them daily, often repeating them mentally in my head. You've already seen some messaging coming through and more will come too. Things happen for you to face your fear. Step into the fear - that is your greatest growth learning to be experienced.

Statements

• You face that fear, and to it, you might say, "Thanks." - "I've got this." - "We've got this." - "I will accept the challenge."

• You become aware that whatever happens you can handle this. "I can handle this, and I can do this." - "I believe in my ability to work things out."

• And remind yourself: In these so-called negative experiences, "There are no mistakes, only learning experiences. I'm a lifelong learner. I am growing and learning."

• If you are disappointed by a certain outcome, remember, "This or something even better is working out."

It's time for stacking lots of goodness in your mind, body and life. The more warm-heartedness and nourishment you have the merrier you can be. You can have such phrases and statements written down, or recorded, somewhere convenient to prompt you. They can be of assistance when feeling some discomfort, concern arising, or if you find your energy or enthusiasm flagging a little. Have them on hand to support you until they become second nature.

Your Thoughts and Your Reality

A lovely lady would say her ex-husband hates her, that was until she realised, she was putting the energy out there and was getting that back. She changed it around and chose her words very carefully and now states: "My ex-husband is learning to accept me."

What are you saying that is no longer serving you? You can do a change around too.

Positive thoughts, create positive intentions, which lead to positive actions.

• The question you can also ask yourself often is, "What is one little thing, one action step, I can do, and do right now?"

It could be as simple as 'change your thinking.' What is a better thought you could have?

Imagine you have access to all the wisdom of all of the sages throughout all-time. Ask and give thanks for this.

You are infinitely and unconditionally loved and supported. You are never alone. The Universe, God, Angels, Guides, Source Energy, Pure Consciousness, or the Unified Field of all the laws of Nature is with you. According to Ram Dass unconditional love really exists in each of us. It is part of our deep inner being. It is not so much an active emotion as a state of being beyond the mind.

Ram Dass, born Richard Alpert (1931-2019), also known as Baba Ram Dass, was an American spiritual teacher, guru of modern yoga, psychologist, and writer. His best-selling 1971 book was *Be Here Now.* In 1997 he had a stroke, which left him with paralysis and unable to speak. He eventually grew to interpret this event as an act of grace, learning to speak again and continuing to teach and write books.

Feel the relief, feel the strength and feel the support. Imagine, if regardless of how things are showing up everything is happening for us, perhaps even as an act of grace.

Remember it's all okay. You're in the right place at the right time.

CHAPTER 3: LIGHTING THE WAY

"Have the courage to follow your heart and intuition, they somehow know what you truly want to become." Steve Jobs

Steve Jobs had a 10-minute rule; Both biographical and scientific evidence point to the fact that, if you're stuck on a hard problem for more than 10 minutes, you should stop beating yourself up at your desk and get up and take a walk instead.

Steven Paul Jobs (1955-2011) was an American businessman, inventor and investor. He was born in San Francisco, California and adopted soon after. He studied Zen Buddhism and wanted to be a monk in Japan. At 21 he co-founded a technology company. That company was Apple Inc. He was also founder of computer company NeXT and chairman and majority shareholder of Pixar Animation Studios. Edwin Catmull and Steve Jobs were the executive producers of the 1995 Disney/Pixar film Toy Story as well.

Lighting the way, you can do this by demonstrating your courage and vision. This is the courage to embrace your new identity as the creator of your reality and to light your way forward. The time is always now, and you get a second chance, or maybe more depending on the situation and people involved. Yes, you might be stepping into uncharted grounds. While some things may seem permanent, nothing is truly certain. The good news is we're in this together and you have more ability than you realise.

This means some of your old ways are dropping off, and often there's a transition period as you adjust. The pendulum swings too far, then it changes direction and eventually returns to its centre. There is an ebb and flow, a natural rhythm of movement occurring. Ideas, thoughts and feelings may be coming up, testing your resolve, as you proceed. This could be unsettling, scary, frustrating, fascinating, empowering, exhilarating. Take Courage.

Inner Intelligence

You can tap into your inner intelligence, that unique mind-brain-body system that each person has. Here within this book are tools and resources available that you can use to go even further with accessing and utilising this ability as well. Listen to your inner wisdom and use it to navigate your life with more ease and peaceful feelings. You can move into new dimensions of a better way of life anchored fully in the heart. Step away from your perceived limitations and enjoy a new speed of energy and clarity. With willingness, compassion and surrendering, you can allow yourself to flow through it all and have a smoother ride. There may be some bumps along the road, but you can handle them too. Knowledge is wisdom applied, use all that we have gained for our betterment from ancient wisdom to our modern times. Let's integrate and activate the best of it all.

Disruption and Distractions

Let's start with your biggest distraction and as Brian Tracy would say, "Let's eat that frog," one bite at a time. As I do love animals and nature my intention is not for you to take this literally, it's a euphemism for tackling your hairiest biggest roadblocks first, one bite, or one step at a time. He said, "If you have to eat two frogs, eat the ugliest one first." This was another way of saying that if you have two important tasks before you, start with the most important (and often hardest) one first.

Brian Tracy is a Canadian/American motivational public speaker and self-development author who has helped millions of business owners around the world. He is the author of over eighty books that have been translated into dozens of languages. One of the books he is best known for is, *Eat That Frog! He* would say you cannot control what happens to you, but you can control your attitude toward what happens to you, and in that, you will be mastering change rather than allowing it to master you. Another quote of his was, "Winners make a habit of manufacturing their own positive expectations in advance of the event."

How are you managing disruptions and distractions? You may find yourself in fast paced times with a lot of external demands competing for your attention and energy. Overstimulation is occurring, especially if one is spending too much time on digital devices. Is this having a negative effect on you, your relationships, or are other areas of your life suffering consequently? This could be addressed by starting up your devices later in the morning or turning them off earlier at night. You could even allocate lunch time as a device free time.

Never underestimate the simplicity of the practice of just taking that next action step and doing it - "today." Then you could wake up the next day and say, "I'm just doing it for today." Keep doing this for the next 30 days and see if just "doing it for today" relieves the pressure. Some of these habits are addictive and making the change one day at a time, in smaller bites can help.

It's time to get present and be aware of what you are choosing and why. No hiding behind old excuses, regardless how validated they may be, no blaming, no beating yourself up, but rising. "If your compassion does not include yourself, it is incomplete." Jack Kornfield. He commented that it never occurred to him to be compassionate with himself, saying, "I am my own worst critic, and I suspect that many of you have the same struggle."

Jack Kornfield has worked as a peacemaker and activist, organised teacher training, and led international gatherings of Buddhist teachers including the Dalai Lama. He is an American writer and teacher as well. Of Jewish descent he is also a fraternal twin. His father was a scientist, which brought him to an interest in healing, medicine and science. He took a course in Asian philosophy and ended up majoring in Asian studies. After graduating College in 1967, Kornfield joined the Peace Corps and was sent to Thailand where he worked on tropical medicine teams in the Mekong River valley. There he met and became a monk.

Your Journey

You're on this journey, in the next stage, phase or chapter of your life. You're here implementing some more good habits and actions, perhaps just doing some tweaks, all to match the next best version of the best you that you can be.

Questions to ask yourself:

• What is required to be of service here?

• How can I grow into that?

Directing and Director

 Write your answers down and take one small action toward that now and feel proud of yourself. You are directing and the director of your new future self.

In 'Directing,' you are guiding or overseeing your life, making creative decisions and instructing the actors in it.

As the 'Director,' you are responsible for this process, the creative leader bringing your vision to life working with the cast and crew to execute it.

May you choose to feel fully engaged in the process. Be present and enjoy your next steps even if they're uncomfortable at first. Your next level of fulfilment and satisfaction await. They are beyond the fears of ruin, it being too hard, rejection, and regret. These are the familiar hallmarks of dissatisfaction and disappointment that can challenge us daily. Reach beyond this now and train yourself to pivot, knowing positive outcomes exist.

Pivot

Silently in your mind, or speaking out loud, you can say:

• "I am connected. I am safe. All is well. I choose the next right action for me. I know I can." Let's do this.

Some people when forming new habits feel uncertain and require an accountability partner, to keep them on track. Some people are questioners and need clarity in their own minds of the benefits of these actions and why they are doing them. Some are rebellious and want to do it their own way.

We're all creators, so finding the way that works best for you, whether it is solo, or bringing on a team. There's no right or wrong way, just your way that works for you with no harm to yourself or others during this process.

I'd like to provide you with two similar quotes as you pivot:

1. "If we always do what we've always done, we always get what we've always gotten."

2. "If you think like you've always thought, you'll continue to get what you've always got."

The message: If you are not changing your mindset or actions and still expecting a different result, it could be time to go a little outside your comfort zone and try a few different tactics and strategies. This can be a pretty awesome journey. What if you are better than you thought you were?

Unblocking Joy and Abundance

I was working with a very switched-on teacher and trainer, who felt they had blocked their abundance. When we discussed what abundance meant for them, what it looked like, what it felt like, one of the feelings was "joy." When they shared the many things that gave them joy, they realised they felt that many times every day. A huge aha moment and even some embarrassment ensued as they had forgotten what they knew. They were not blocked from abundance, they just thought they were.

Do you appreciate reminders of what you may already know too? Let's dissolve real or perceived blocks together.

If at first you don't succeed, check in with yourself, as you may fear succeeding this time and blocking yourself from the great things you already know. Yes, you are so much better than you ever imagined!

You will be able to handle whatever comes your way, even if you haven't in the past. You are not who you were. You now have more skills, resources and changed belief systems. Let these serve you for your highest good. They're here for you - put them on, use them.

If you can be willing to step into the realm of infinite possibilities and the quantum field of all that is, you will come across a huge warehouse of answers, solutions that are right for you.

A slightly overweight restaurateur decided that he was going to be an Olympian. He showed us this power of possibility. Those around him scoffed at the idea, but he had belief in himself and the focus on what he needed to do to achieve this. Three years later he was in the British team competing at Athens in the shooting event.

Nudges

Your life is unfolding. How would you like this next chapter to be?

What would it look like or feel like, if you envisioned the dreams and desires you have, as yours now?

If you already have this awareness, or not, whether you are ready to embrace it or not, life is ready for you. Ready for the magnificent you that you were born into this world to be.

No matter how hard you try to ignore something, the more you resist your true path, the more it will nudge you.

At first it is gentle, quietly reminding you to show up in a better way, a better light, and a brighter light. I like the quote that Colette Baron Reid uses as her go to:

• "Whatever is meant for you, will not pass you."

Colette Baron-Reid is a Canadian writer, public speaker, spiritual medium and oracle card reader.

Your nudging knows no boundaries. It's always easier to get the message earlier; otherwise, some of the nudging may not be such a nice experience for you.

Are you choosing to love your life, learn in life and get good at both? Sometimes the learning hurts, so get good at your own personal journey and those lessons. Release old fears, as they too have passed.

Are you ready to allow that, and keep allowing that? This is part of the surrendering into the new self and the new world that is unfolding. We're still in our infancy, so just like a baby taking its first steps, you may stumble a little. Nothing wrong with that, as long as you keep moving, moving into more love, more light, more unity, more peace, more joy, more compassion, more forgiveness, more fun. That's not a bad start on stepping into your new version of your best self.

Reflecting

Ponder on this:

• "If everything that comes to us is a reflection of us, how differently would you perceive people and life?"

For some a nudge could be as dramatic as an accident. A high achieving career guy had this happen to him. He already knew he needed to be more present with his family, and was making great strides in achieving this, but his work was really pressing on him and a lot of mental fatigue and strain was being experienced.

He couldn't lighten up as much as he truly desired on the work front, that was until he had the accident. He suddenly had clarity on what was really important and was able to shift his attitude and habits to succeed at both. This is an ongoing practice and process, which becomes easier as you do the actions to match your true intentions.

Clarity

Who are you, what are your patterns and what are your gifts to learn?

• Are you a Lightworker?

• Are you an Empath?

You don't have to be either of these or you don't even have to already know what they are. You instead may realise some beautiful similarities that you already possess. You can choose to integrate these and other qualities that serve you, others and humanity well. No labelling is required, you are you, you are unique, and we want you to show up as only you can.

When seeking clarity ask yourself does this information help, hinder, soothe, or cause more suffering? For your choices in life, what is your own highest good where you are doing no harm to yourself, or others?

The traits of a Lightworker:

• Feel called to heal others.

•Want to resolve the world's social and environmental problems.

Descriptions of Empaths:

• Empaths are affected by other people's energies and have an innate ability to intuitively feel and perceive others.

• They just know stuff, without being told. It's a knowing that goes way beyond intuition or gut feelings, even though that is how many would describe the knowing. The more attuned and connected the stronger this gift becomes for you.

Other areas you may identify with:

• Do you strive for the truth, answers and knowledge and notice that anything untruthful feels plain wrong?

• Do you like adventure, freedom and travel? Are you a free spirit?

• Are you an excellent listener? Do you find that you don't talk about yourself much, unless it's to someone you really trust? "I love to learn and know about others and genuinely care."

Regardless of your traits, please feel that you have a home here too.

Healing Your Life

Louise Hay has a symptoms list and the meanings behind it in her book: *You Can Heal Your Life,* which is a great companion to have. You can also go online and get the list, which can be another helpful unveiling.

An example of one of these symptoms is digestive disorders and lower back problems:

• The solar plexus chakra is based in the centre of the abdomen, and it's known as the seat of emotions. This is where many can feel the incoming emotion of another, which can weaken the area and eventually lead to anything from stomach ulcers to irritable bowel syndrome.

This is looking from another perspective and can be part of the equation to give you further insights and possibilities to reclaim or enhance your health and wellbeing. If you have a curious mind like I do, it can take your knowledge to another level of awareness. This can be a fun fascinating journey.

There is an A-Z of conditions covered in Louise's book. You can check out the list she has online. Another interesting example she shares is that lower back problems can develop from being ungrounded, amongst other things.

How do I get grounded? Walking barefoot on grass, sand, or soil, or even barefoot in your home.

Some other next steps include a system called root cause analysis. This is where one identifies potential causes, determines which are the roots and addresses those causes to ensure the problem does not recur. This is done by asking the questions How/What/Why five times. It is said to be a highly effective process. Most of us stop at about 2 or 3 of the "Why" questions thinking we already have the right answer.

This is not to replace the assistance you choose from your health care provider. May you continue getting optimal nutrition, sleep and exercise too.

Clutter

This is another aspect that is great to look at as well. Clutter in your mind, your home, your life. You can feel weighed down and your flow of energy can be blocked when you have too much clutter. In your home de-clutter and keep what you love. It could be section by section. A great section to start with is your clothes. What sparks joy? Out of 10 tops, what are your top 3? It's okay, you can keep more than 3. Keep moving, keep clearing and keep asking what do I really love, and what is useful? Love it and have a use for it in the next 12 months. What is that use? State it, name it, love it, or thank it, and let it go.

Clutter can also be in the form of a cluttered life, trying to do too much. A cluttered diary, always too busy is one of the symptoms.

- What are you busy doing?

- How important is that?

- Why is that so important?

You could even continue and go deeper. Going deeper by asking 5 why's and uncover a root cause. In doing this you may find the real reason behind the clutter. As you explore this check-in as to how true that reason or belief is for you now. You might be pleasantly surprised about what you can now let go of.

What can you let go of?

If all your possessions were suddenly removed, yes all of them, clothes, jewellery, furniture, phones... What would be the first 21 things you'd want back and why?

Gratitude

There are so many things to be grateful for and it's a powerful practice to cultivate. Some of the benefits include reducing anxiety, anger, allowing more contentment and resilience. As we reflect on the things we are grateful for daily we can be peppering this appreciation throughout our days. Morning, noon and night, loving and appreciating what we already have and allowing more goodness in. When you can't summon a genuine feeling for gratitude and it seems superficial, allow the contrast, feel what you feel, notice your body. We're doing this thankfulness to trigger happy hormones in the brain and activate the feel-good vibes. You'll hear gratitude, love and appreciation as cornerstones of many great practices throughout the ages. These practices can support you in finding your best ways forward too.

Part of My Journey

I grew up seeing the simplicity of life enjoyed so much by my Grandparents and their love of nature. They were not into the material world. They were a stabilising influence when the pull of the world was advertising something new and shiny, that "you really must have."

We lived remotely, and there was a big world out there for me to explore. I chose to seek adventure and travel. What was the rest of the world like? I wanted to find out for myself. This shocked many as they saw me growing up as a timid sensitive child.

My desire was strong, and I took on many roles to earn and save money to achieve my goals. I heard the voices of those who didn't make it very far, or for very long, so I learnt through them. I spent time working and travelling to build up my resources.

Australia was my first port of call on this extended overseas travel, checking in if I was cut out for this exploration. I decided that if I wasn't, I wouldn't be stuck too far away, or without the money to return home. I had a compass and a set point in that I knew I could always find joy in the simplicity of life as well.

For me my wonder lust continued, I asked myself, "how did the rest of the world really tick?"

That kept the fire in my belly to travel and see this world. How exciting to see and explore first hand. How did others live? What were these people and places like? Why did they think and act in such ways? I was here to understand, learn and appreciate the melting pot of life, including myself so much more.

When I returned from my travels, still in my early 20's, I chose to continue exploring, including ancient Eastern philosophy. I looked at what was considered some of the most elevated and important of all spiritual knowledge. Here I also found huge volumes of scientific evidence to support the claims. Science and nature, these two elements can provide foundations for us. This can mean when you hear other collaborating evidence, you can look to these elements and beyond the visible to find answers. You can be more trusting of your own innate abilities and discover or rediscover them too.

Direction

Remember you don't have to know or do this. Marilyn Alauria, a Psychic Medium, Teacher and Coach prefers not to know to keep the purity of the messages coming through. This way her analytical thinking mind doesn't start making up or adding new stories to distort the message. Marilyn is also the Creator of "Next Level Living" and host of the "Who Can It Be Now" podcast.

Theories in science are always being reconsidered, so let's reconsider and explore your abilities:

• What do you already know?

• What do you not yet know?

Flowers blossom, the sun shines and stars sparkle, understand the interconnectedness of it all. Trust yourself and your instincts. You can have your feet firmly grounded in Mother Earth, *Gaia, or however you like to describe the ground beneath your feet and also have that invisible thread reaching into the cosmos of all that is.

*Gaia, in Greek mythology is the ancestral mother of all life.

Use this to imagine, imagine how joy-filled your life is and can be. You can do this and have a deep knowing too. Why/ How, because for whatever reason you were led to be reading or hearing this book now. You are powerful.

Sometimes you will see it is a path you have walked before and at other times you will be curious to understand more of what another does or believes to be the way. This does not mean you then become brainwashed and begin a dangerous or harmful way of life. You have a road map, and as you choose the way that is personalised for you for your highest good, you start a knowing of what feels right and wrong.

If your path is not feeling right, take a measure of where you are at and where you want to head. Talk to others who seem to be where you want to be and discuss the journey. You might be near the light at the end of that tunnel, or it may be time to take another path?

How strong is your desire, what is your vision and deep knowing? If you don't know, what could it be?

Momentum

The strength or force gained by motion. Looking for the simplicity in the complexity and taking the next best step. What interests you? List all the things you like, like to do, or would like to do. You could see this as your bucket list or create this onto your vision board full of pictures and words or record it too. Do not be concerned if there are activities and items that others get a lot of satisfaction and joy from, and you don't, or it doesn't work out so great. This is your new list, a fresh start, one that feels really good for you. Then check in, are your actions aligning with who you are now becoming? This includes the character traits you most admire and appreciate too. Going into this next chapter of your life being and bringing out your best.

For what interests you, one lady wrote down "to join a dance class." She had been recommended one that was very good. She boldly purchased a 10-session card and after attending a couple she was thinking, "it's not really my thing" and decided she would see out the 10 classes and then not renew. The more she went however, the more she got to know others and started liking the classes, feeling more competent and in so doing, more confident. A few years later she is still attending the classes and has a beautiful group of new friends she adores.

Never underestimate the momentum and joy that can come from doing 1 good thing a day. It could be the momentum that can be gained from choosing something that interests you and simply continuing like the story above. It could also be from what I like to call, "the 1 press-up formula." I've been practicing this for a few years now.

The One Press-up Formula

For me it started with 1 press-up a day. People would laugh and think why bother? It's too easy and for that reason many felt it wasn't worth doing.

What they didn't realise is that when you choose to act in this easy, sustainable way, your natural tendency is to do just 1 more.

My 1 press up is not 1 or 2, but normally 11.

What if I choose to skip a day? I'm still way ahead than I ever expected to be, and it was easy. What motivates me to continue this habit?

Being healthy at 100 is one reason, and to achieve that, I take action to support this outcome now. Exercise is part of the MEDS formula: Meditation, Exercise, Diet, Sleep. Healthy at 100 means living a lifestyle that allows one to be physically and mentally healthy even at the age of 100. I realise some people do not want to live to that age or believe they can. Whatever age we do reach, how does maximising our Healthspan sound so we enjoy our life even more? The goal: Living a vibrant life with minimal health complications.

I also feel that I have strong toned arms because of this, it's a win-win and I am grateful. See where you can extend the power of one. As you do this, consider what can you do in "one" minute? Act and do it now.

These little things have a compounding effect and, in the process, clear a lot for you. The road ahead is one of discovery, perhaps even recovery. These techniques are also great for those who procrastinate. I generally find hard wired procrastinators do very well having an accountability partner, whether that is a friend, a group, a personal coach, or all the above.

"It's not the mountain we conquer, but ourselves." Sir Edmund Hillary

On 29 May 1953 Edmund Hillary, a New Zealand mountaineer and explorer, and Nepalese Sherpa mountaineer, Tenzing Norgay became the first confirmed climbers to reach the summit of Mount Everest.

Regardless of where you've been and what mountains you've had to climb, there is light and a space of unbounded love and support available for you too. Your next chapter - Light the way.

Remember it's all okay. You're in the right place at the right time.

CHAPTER 4: SUCCESS SETTINGS

"Don't judge each day by the harvest you reap, but by the seeds that you plant." Robert Louis Stevenson

Robert Louis Stevenson (1850-1894) was a Scottish novelist, essayist, poet and travel writer. His first successful novel, *Treasure Island* was published in 1884. His other best-known work was *The Strange Case of Dr Jekyll and Mr Hyde.*

I visited the grave of this famous Scottish writer high on a hill in tropical Samoa. It was a long, hot, steep climb, but we persevered and were rewarded with a cool breeze and magnificent view at the top. Success.

When we look for the 6 top tips to set us up for success, we may ponder and ask ourselves these 3 questions.

1. What am I wanting?

2. Why do I want this?

3. If it was already so, what seeds would I now be planting to achieve it?

At this stage you may be thinking these top tips are straight forward, and we are often reminded of 3 key things.

1. Don't give up.

2. Don't take anything personally.

3. And if it is so important, don't take no for an answer.

"The people who told me no were the people who eventually told me yes." That was a quote from the fastest growing retailer in 2012, Nasty Gal vintage clothing founder Sophia Amoruso.

For me, the 'not taking no for an answer,' is about us becoming better with traits like conscientiousness and persistency. It's also finding other ways forward. This may mean they eventually come to us, saying yes, but it isn't about hassling people, so they do.

Four Guideposts

Tools to Use:

1. Follow your heart as opposed to following the money. "When we follow the things we love most, those things we are most passionate about, we're able to spend more time, put in more detail and thoughtfulness, into making them come to life." Lewis Howes. Entrepreneur and former professional football player.

   As you get grounded in your heart and are planting seeds of more success, prepare the earth for the best growing environment. Get yourself in the right state to help you feel more relaxed and calmer.

2. The Physiological Sigh. A physiological sigh is a breathing pattern that involves two inhales and a long exhale. It's a deep breath that can help reduce stress and anxiety. Inhale through your nose twice, filling your lungs almost to capacity. The second inhale opens the air sacs in your lungs. Exhale slowly through your mouth, releasing excess carbon dioxide.

   Andrew Huberman an American neuroscientist, and associate professor of neurobiology and ophthalmology at the Stanford University School of Medicine, says this: The physiological sigh - two deep inhales through the nose (no exhale in between), followed by a full exhale to empty lungs (through the mouth) is the fastest way to reduce autonomic arousal, aka "calm down", and causes activation of neural circuits specifically for calming. Since 2021, he has hosted the popular health and science focused

Huberman Lab podcast.

3. Heart. Do the Physiological Sigh and breathe through your heart; breathe love, appreciation, compassion, courage, calm, confidence and connection.

4. Presence. Choose to stay present, awake, aware and fully engaged.

Are you willing and ready to adjust, adapt and improve your current settings. How about following your true heart's desires?

To avoid suffering burnout in the process, here are the 6 top tips to build a strong foundation for success.

The 6 Top Tips for Building a Strong Foundation:

1. 7-8 hrs of sleep per night.

2. Some form of yoga, tai-chi and movement, exercising 20 minutes per day at least three times a week.

3. Meditation, mindfulness, faith: stress management.

4. Healthy relationships, with yourself, others and connecting with nature, the earth.

5. Eating fresh nourishing food, preferably organic, spray free. Ideally eliminating processed foods.

6. Drinking fresh unadulterated water every day.

Remember these are only tips, not rules. We want you to thrive without pressure, so if you start by acting on some of these that is fine too.

The "kaizen" approach is widely used throughout the world. It is the Japanese word for continual improvement.

Use these tips and tools to assist you, so you can continually improve in the areas that matter most to you now.

Awareness of your: Mind. Body. Soul. Heart.

Allowing yourself to be: Centred. Happy. Strong. Clear. Energetic.

Courageously moving forward. On purpose. Your bases covered. Your foundations strong.

Listen to Your Body

The popular HIIT - High Intensity Interval Training: short, e.g. 30-second fast blasts of intense exercise with brief rests have some great benefits. Including weight resistance exercises are high on the list to do. As you age this type of exercise from squats to press ups, to other forms that serve your body well can be very beneficial.

Seek Out the Advice You Require

5 Exercise Tips and Possibilities:

1. Employ a personal trainer and build up your body.

2. A regime that includes a couple of days of weight resistance and a couple of days of some form of cardio exercise.

3. For females, from about 20 years old, your bladder will thank you for including pelvic floor exercises too.

4. Achieving the 10,000 steps a day as part of your cardio target for wellbeing.

5. If you're an elite athlete, choose your regime and team to work smarter and more effectively at your next level of brilliance.

I did the HIIT for a couple of years, then stopped. It was no longer resonating with my body, so I moved forward with other exercises, exploring what now brought it joy. The door can open and close for what is now right for us. I have found different versions of the HIIT that can feel good for me. You keep the space open for what is currently best for you and your body.

Awareness of Feelings

Be aware of the feelings you want to give and receive.

• What can you be excited and enthused about today?

• What are the outcomes you want to achieve today?

• With these questions in mind, ask yourself: "What are my next right actions to feel fulfilled and satisfied here?"

You could be feeling excited and inspired already, or you could have that sinking feeling and insecurities. You may be thinking much of this is common knowledge but remember that does not always translate into being common practice. You can choose to feel re-inspired rather than a bit down about it. Be prepared to let go and release old energies and beliefs that have held you back in the past.

Breath. Heart. Presence. In your power. You've got it. Are you ready to do this now?

• Feel into the relief of this and do more of what lights you up consistently. Once you've achieved success in one area, come back and repeat the process in your next area, and then the next, and next.

• Feel proud of what you are doing and where you are heading.

• What is one to do or start doing now. What aspects can you achieve, or complete quite quickly?

You think of the bigger picture of what lights you up and that you find fulfilling. Feel into all the benefits of creating this. What is the good that can come from you stepping into your power and what command have you to make it happen?

Can you do this by yourself, or will you enrol another to assist? Some may have illness or injury factors and engage the services of a team of experts, collaborators, whomever and whichever way is right for you. You have the power to choose.

Now bring your future vision back into this present moment and allow yourself to feel good about it. Feel some relief too. Feel good here in this space taking inspired actions and then straight after having achieved your goal, reflect and feel good again about what you are doing and who you are becoming in the process. Setting your mind and body up with good feelings to keep moving ahead is a great practice. This is like habit stacking which can help reduce stress and anxiety and increase motivation and discipline. It can have many other benefits, including improving confidence, building resilience, and developing cognitive skills. Using existing habits to build new ones can help you feel more confident and motivated too. Being open-minded can help you feel less pressured to be perfect and embrace everything life has to offer.

Bring More of Your Joy

If you feel there is something holding you back, what are the underlying beliefs that could be limiting the incredible you, what are you pretending, what stories are you telling yourself that are holding you back from how great you really are and can be? What if you chose to create more joy, be more joy, see more joy.

Whatever comes up truth or not, write it down, you might be surprised at what comes up as you reflect on your current beliefs. The next step is to ask: "How true is that now," on a 1-10 scale?

The common theme I notice when I provide reflection tests is how the light of awareness and insight can easily shine and how little changes can make a big difference.

The businessman whose relationships were scoring lower wanted a closer connection with his daughters. He shared how proud he was of them. The question I asked is have you told them that? He hadn't.

- What can you do now?

- What is important for you?

Just because you may have failed at something in the past, that perceived failure does not need to dictate your future.

For me I was doing a pretty good job of keeping my ducks in a row and following that 6-point formula, but despite that, something was still missing, and maybe that's how you feel sometimes too? Take another look.

Your Environment and Home

- 1. You've de-cluttered and noticed how much lighter and freer you've become in this process. You've lessened stagnant energy, you're feeling better. You're continually adjusting your success settings to a higher realm.

- 2. There is also the "sick home syndrome," which can be caused by mould spores, ley lines and geopathic stress. You can learn how to balance out these and other issues or get someone in to clear them for you.

- 3. You've ensured your home is well ventilated and you allow fresh air to flow through.

- 4. You've removed toxins and chemicals that are causing harm. This may be cleaning or personal care items, it also may be toxic relationships. Set clear boundaries. Seek the support you may need.

As a new mum I recall learning and reciting the 40 *Sanskrit phrases to myself. I could play with this, creating a space of more peace, harmony and yes perhaps even restful sleep. It was not the normal thing a *kiwi girl would do then, or now.

The *Sanskrit words I was repeating explore the branches of Ayurveda and have a resonance on our planet. Ayurveda means the study of life. It takes a natural approach to all aspects of health and well-being. Ayurvedic medicine (Ayurveda for short) is one of the world's oldest holistic (whole body) healing systems. It was developed more than 3,000 years ago in India. It's based on the belief that health and wellness depend on a delicate balance between the mind, body, and spirit.

*Kiwi is the nickname for a New Zealander and is derived from our national symbol of our native flightless bird - The Kiwi.

Movement of the body is a great way to reset and clear cluttered thoughts. Many experts recommend a 20 minute walk each day. This is not on a treadmill inside, but outside in nature, getting that fresh air to clear the mind and get the creative juices flowing.

Learning, understanding and knowing how to support your wellbeing are great tools for your toolbox. There are also many other healing modalities. Some of these I will cover in this book, others you may discover yourself. You might even find you go beyond these current needs and requirements and simply be great, knowing you are that already. Follow your inner wisdom and enjoy optimal wellbeing, a natural extension of who you are.

Keep in Mind

• What is your goal?

• What belief systems are you willing to let go of?

Each time you read, or hear this book, notice how much further you have come. Notice how you are receiving another level of tools and insights. You're ready for more. Step away from the noise and into the stillness of your wisdom. Sometimes that only takes a second. You can then carry on renewed, excited and enthused. From silence to dynamism, yes you are amazing.

The Success Setting of Food

Let's take a deeper look at what we put into and onto our bodies:

Do you wish to know what the ingredients are in the food you buy? A simple rule is - less is best. If there are too many ingredients that you do not recognise, or numbers that don't make sense, maybe this is not what you want to consume. Ideally, we will be simply guided to the food that is best for us and eat mindfully. Enjoy the smell, taste, textures and look of the food as you eat. Enjoy the environment you are in too.

If you'd like to understand some more, I find it helpful to know a few extra tips and insights for when reading food labels.

Sugar: 1 teaspoon of sugar is 4.2 grams. A 4-gram conversion can be used to understand how much sugar is in a food product. Foods containing more than 10 grams (just over 2 teaspoons) of added sugars per serving is high. Keep your intake lower than this to avoid major sugar spikes and crashes.

Salt: 1 teaspoon of table salt is about 6 grams. When reading labels and looking at added salt (sodium) in a product, the preference is less than 120mg per 100 grams. Foods that are 100-600 mg per 100 grams are considered okay, but recommendations are to go for less. Some say foods with more than 400mg per 100mg should be avoided if possible. Others also say that Adults should have no more than 6g of salt a day (around 1 level teaspoon). This includes the salt that's already in our food and the salt added during and after cooking.

For me it is about quality and purity. I'm also mindful of iodine deficiencies. Harvard Health Publishing stated in their article, "Cut salt it won't affect your iodine intake" June 1, 2011; "Iodised salt provides only a small fraction of daily iodine intake."

Seaweed (kelp, nori, wakame) and eggs are rich sources of iodine. Prunes and lima beans can be a good source for those who do not eat fish, eggs, or dairy.

If you're not quite there yet and want some more practical information you can use, here are a couple of examples of ingredients that are best not to consume:

• High Fructose Corn Syrup (HFCS): The refined sugar we consume may be declining, but this has been increasing, and it is said to increase triglycerides, boost fat-storing hormones, and drives people to overeat and gain weight.

• Palm Oil: When a regular fat like corn, soybean, or palm oil is blasted with hydrogen and turned into a solid, it becomes a trans-fat. Tans-fats help packaged foods stay "fresh," so they can sit on shelves without rotting, or getting stale. They are said to raise your "bad" LDL cholesterol and triglycerides and lowers your "good" HDL. Fried foods are usually fried in one of these, so best not to consume either.

This can be too big a subject to fully digest here, hence keep it simple. The mantra I follow is the less processed foods you consume the better.

Shortening, or partially hydrogenated oil is an ingredient, this is classed as a trans-fat. You are not here to clog your arteries and cause obesity. Choose other oils instead, such as olive oil. Unsaturated omega 3 fatty acids are getting the nod too. For high heat you may like coconut oil, avocado oil, ghee, or even a little water. Sesame and peanut oil are also recommended for those without nut allergies. Keep in mind the oils and foods you choose are pesticide free. Read words like organic, extra virgin and cold pressed on your oil labels.

Saturated fats get such a bad rap, but slowly the understanding is becoming clear; trans-fats are the things for you to eat less of. Use and enjoy non-genetically modified foods too. Little changes like sea salt rather than table salt can also serve you well.

You're not after artificial sweeteners, colours, flavours in your foods either. Replacing processed grains, the white flour, rice, pasta and bread with whole grains like brown or wild rice, whole-wheat breads and pastas, barley and oatmeal can be a smart thing to do as well.

Alkalising your body: It is strongly suggested that too many bodies, particularly those with Western diets are acidic and this can cause a host of health challenges. This affects your brain, bones, lungs, heart, liver, pancreas, and kidneys, intestines, stomach and skin.

Here are some common alkali ash foods. These foods help to control the acid in your internal environment: spinach, cucumber, broccoli, avocado, celery and almonds. Fortunately, there are lots more.

Understanding food and its effects on you is a fascinating undertaking. The humble watermelon has diuretic properties, which means an increase in the amount of water and salt expelled from the body as urine. That can be good in some circumstances, working on your kidneys and blood pressure, whereas too many diuretic foods may not be ideal when the skin shows the need for rejuvenation and replenishing.

You are in a time of the latest superfoods being the answer to all your problems, but food is an individual personalised approach. It's time to really listen to your body and notice what it loves and when.

Watermelon is interestingly rated number 11 of a top 25 superfoods list in 2012. For me eating a sweet orange, or blood orange can offer excellent nutritional benefits to my body. Another day or season the watermelon might serve me well. The important reminder is it doesn't have to feature on the superfood list, to provide you with the nourishment your body desires.

Listening to Your Body

 Listen to your body, as you eat and afterwards too. Be aware of the seasons, the country you are in, and its fresh local produce. It's okay if your body doesn't love and adore the foods you have been told should be good for you, there are plenty of others to explore. Sometimes it's simply having a great variety of cooked or fresh unprocessed foods. Having the colours of the rainbow and that doesn't mean M&M's (chocolate candy) on your dinner plate. Switch things around, more of one, less of another, for your best nourishment and wellbeing.

Having a strong digestive fire or Agni (fire) means your body can make the most use of the food for nourishing your body. As you give your car an oil and lubrication each year, doing a detox that's right for your biotype can be a very smart move also.

As you exercise your trust muscle, exercise your body as well. The endorphins from movement and exercise, along with nourishing whole foods fed into your body, are setting you up for success.

Know yourself and your shortfalls, those times you may slip back and do habits that are not truly nourishing your mind, body, soul. If you do backslide, simply learn from this experience, go back to your set point (love and kindness in awareness) and change it up.

Did you really slip back, backslide and buckle under pressure or temptation, or were you not prepared enough to set yourself up for success? Note it is normally the latter. How can you counterbalance this?

The solution can be preparing things in advance. Whether it is having easily accessible good food in the pantry, or healthful snacks for those drops in energy, you may experience of an afternoon. The better you fuel your body; the less afternoon dips you will encounter.

Allow yourself to be guided. Ask for the highest and best in you to come through, just like you were guided to choose to read, or listen to this book. Allow so much good to come through you, for you and all those you love. There are a lot of strategies and things on this planet for you to explore.

Remember this information is to support you in making great choices that are right for you and your wellbeing. Whatever food or thoughts you are taking in, love that, and trust that you are receiving everything you need for vibrant health, even if at times it may not seem so.

Love the food that loves you back.

Too many people eat something knowing and saying it's not good or healthy for them. Instead of being so self-critical of yourself, transition into better healthier ways of self-talk as well.

Messages

 You could speak out or say to yourself:

• "I choose this. I appreciate the nourishment I am receiving from it."

• "I am so grateful that my body transmutes everything into its highest form of vitality for me."

• "I release all guilt and fear. I love and appreciate who I am. Thank you."

• "I am eternally grateful."

Food/Diet

As I researched nutrition/food/diet, I also saw how it provoked strong reactions with a diverse range of diets and perspectives. Some groups felt their one was the way. Here's a sampling: Mediterranean, Paleo, Intermittent fasting, Keto, Plant-based, Vegan, Vegetarian, Flexitarian, Low-carb, Carnivore, Blood type and Raw food. With respect and honouring each person's journey I explored deeper.

It reminded me of the hornets' nest my husband and I walked into when we were in Niue. It was easy to accidentally stir things up. Unbeknown to us the nest had fallen onto the walking track.

We did provoke a strong reaction. We were also grateful that on our return trip we knew where they were. We had walked this path and were able to navigate it so that we didn't provoke them or receive any more stings. We had deeper awareness and knowledge which helped us on the rest of that journey. May what I share here assist you well as you make your best way forward too and awaken the healer within.

It seemed there was some common ground, none of these diets were promoting diets high in white flour and white sugar and lots of processed foods. According to the Interviews Jonathan Landsman was having on the Alzheimer's and Dementia Summit, consuming lots of bread, pasta, sugar, these refined carbohydrates increased the risk of Alzheimer's by 400%.

Natural Health 365

Jonathan has been in the health and fitness industry for over 35 years and host of NaturalHealth365.com. His intent is to be revealing the very best information in science and natural health solutions. He has created over 500 online programmes with over 300 of the brightest minds in natural health and science. He is the creator of 5 best-selling online educational programmes including the Cardiovascular and Fatty Liver Docu-Class. His Summits and Docu-classes I have watched include those on Diabetes, Holistic Oral Health, Alzheimer's and Dementia, Immune Defense, Lung Health, Cardiovascular, Kidney and the Stop Cancer, to name some.

Itis

I was also reminded of the term –itis, this means inflammation. Health conditions ending in 'itis' have inflammation occurring. The good news is you can do something to decrease it without adverse side effects. Examples are Arthritis, Bronchitis, Diverticulitis, Dermatitis.

Many find good quality Omega 3 fatty acids helpful, cleaning up their diet, their personal care products, meditating and exercising. These people were getting back on track. I was seeing them getting happier and healthier simply by utilising more of these foundational tools. By tapping into the wisdom available, finding out what they did not yet know, I saw them successfully implementing another level of healthier habits and lives.

The Food Revolution Network, Inc.

Ocean Robbins and his dad, John Robbins, co-founded this California-based company. His dad followed the call of his conscience and walked away from the Baskin-Robbins fortune and family business. He paved his own way and went to seek greater purpose and meaning in life beyond the Ice cream empire. Their site has a lot of informative blogs answering many commonly asked questions with good evaluations. They advocate a whole foods, plant-based diet.

Current Preferences

I continue to study, experiment and research to find the best ways forward. I found the Ayurvedic way of eating, with its emphasis being a diet of whole foods, fresh organic produce, whole grains, legumes, nuts, seeds, herbs, spices, utilising seasonal ingredients appealed. It's generally vegetarian, but meat can be included in moderation. If tolerated dairy foods like milk, yoghurt and soft cheeses like panir. The milk was heated for 5-10 minutes with spices to change its molecular structure, so it was more digestible. To eat in a way that supports good digestion was important. The ideal gap between two meals according to Ayurveda is four to five hours as it allows the body to completely digest and absorb the nutrients. It also focuses on your unique mind-body type, also known as a dosha.

The Three Main Dosha's:

1. Kapha. Kapha is a water dosha which governs stability, structure and moisture in the body and mind.
2. Pitta. Pitta is a fire dosha and controls digestion and metabolism.

3. Vata. Vata is the wind dosha which controls movement, the nervous system, and waste elimination.

I enjoy the combination of this knowledge and American Doctor, Nutritional Researcher Joel Fuhrman's.

Nutritarian

Joel Fuhrman calls his way a Nutritarian diet. It's a whole foods plant-based diet emphasising nutrient-dense micro-nutrient rich foods which are naturally lower in calories. This also has a good range of phytonutrients and phytochemicals for optimal wellbeing. It includes a large variety of vegetables, fruits, legumes, nuts, seeds, herbs for a good gut microbiome. What I like about Dr Fuhrman's way is the research for it is based on hard end points, long term large-scale studies of 20 plus years rather than 2 or 3 years. What I noticed was other diets could work for a few years, but then what? I wanted a way of nourishing my body that not only nourished it well now but was proven to prevent and lower the risk of many of our common diseases.

The acronym to go with this way is GBOMBS:

- **Greens**, cruciferous vegetables provide unique phytochemicals (ITCs) with a variety of cancer-fighting effects. Greater consumption of these vegetables is linked to reduced risk of cancer and cardiovascular disease and a longer life.

- **Beans** and other legumes are rich in fibre and resistant starch, which help keep blood glucose, blood pressure, and LDL cholesterol down, promote weight loss, promote colon health, and nourish the microbiome.

- **Onions** and garlic are linked to a reduction in the risk of several cancers, and their distinctive sulfur-containing phytochemicals have a number of actions that benefit the cardiovascular system.

- **Mushroom** Phytochemicals are unique in their promotion of immune system function and their ability to inhibit estrogen production; mushroom consumption is associated with a reduced risk of breast cancer.

- **Berry** Phytochemicals have anti-cancer and blood pressure-lowering effects and are linked to a reduced risk of heart attack. Blueberries have also shown promise for improving brain health, in studies on memory and cognitive function.

- **Seeds** and nuts: Eating nuts regularly is associated with longevity, reduced risk of cardiovascular disease, and a healthy body weight. Different seeds have different nutritional benefits. Flax and chia, for example, are rich in omega-3 ALA and lignans, anti-estrogenic phytochemicals linked to a reduction in breast and prostate cancer risk.

Your Body

Your body is great at absorbing as well. Your skin is the largest organ of your body and since it is porous, it absorbs whatever you put on it. Keep your personal care and home cleaning products simple, biodegradable and toxic free. Some studies have linked cosmetic ingredients to allergic reactions, poisonings, damaged DNA, hormone disruption, and increased cancer risk. Beauty products aren't preapproved before they hit the market. Companies are not required to substantiate safety of these products before they sell them. It's possible to find formaldehyde, a known carcinogen banned in EU-sold cosmetics, in US hair-straightening treatments and nail polish.

Here's a sample of personal care ingredients that you may want to check are not in the products you are purchasing:

• Foaming agents such as Sodium lauryl sulphate (SLS) and Sodium laureth sulphate (SLES), found in shampoos, face wash and shower gels.

• Triclosan, found in soaps and toothpastes.

• Toluene, nail products and hair dyes. It's also listed on the label as benzene, toluol, phenylmethane, or methylbenzene.

• Phthalates found in colour cosmetics, fragranced lotions, body washes, hair care and nail polishes too. This could be on the label as phthalate, DEPO, DPB, DEHP and fragrance.

You're not here to have problematic skin conditions, irritations, hormonal dysfunctions, impaired liver and other vital organ dysfunctions anymore either.

EWG.org the environmental working group were always a good resource. They have a "skindeep" cosmetic database where you can look up the safety of more than 97,000 products and ingredients. These days there is also a free app called "think dirty" and it rates the products 1-10 based on carcinogenicity, developmental and reproductive toxicity and allergies and immunotoxicity.

The European Union (EU) has banned over 2,400 chemicals in cosmetics while the US has outlawed or curbed just 11. The EU regulates cosmetics through the Scientific Committee on Consumer Safety (SCCS). The SCCS provides opinions on the health and safety risks of cosmetic products.

Vinegar, Baking Soda, Essential Oils, Almond Oil, Castor Oil and Coconut Oil (or high-quality carrier oils) are 6 essentials I have in my home, for a wide variety of tasks. Thankfully you are spoilt for choice with healthier alternatives, natural and organic products, effective, affordable and accessible. Get good at reading labels and not just the advertising.

Another reminder in the balancing process is to eat food that is a balance of the 5 tastes. These are:

• Pungent • Sweet • Sour • Astringent • Bitter

You can achieve these tastes with the use of your food and various spices such as, but not limited to - turmeric, ginger, fennel, cumin, coriander, cinnamon, cayenne and black pepper.

Ayurvedic spices enhance digestion and metabolism. They also cleanse ama which is a toxic by product from improper or incomplete digestion from the body. They prevent digestive disorders such as gas and bloating as well. These spices include cinnamon, cardamom, turmeric, cumin, coriander, fennel, dill and mint.

You can use your shopping dollar wisely, feel even better and find you spend less in the long run on your overall wellbeing too. You can look after the environment and support local small businesses that are showing care to and for your planet. You can also support larger companies who are ethical and doing the right thing by you, for your body and the environment.

Making it Happen

• Break it down into manageable bites.

• Review your progress, each week.

• What have I done well, and what can I do even better?

If you have takeaways once a week, start stretching that out to once a month. Bring in more variety as well.

Do you have the same breakfast most mornings? Start varying it by exploring other foods that can be nourishing for you.

I'll whip up interesting oat and lentil combinations, different smoothies, using fruits, vegetables, nuts, seeds and spices. That wasn't always the way, as a kid I had quite a sweet tooth. I grew up with, "meat and 3 veg," a standard Kiwi (New Zealand) diet. My understanding then was food was fuel.

"Everything in moderation, was a healthy diet." I found out that statement gives us permission to eat less-nutritious food more often and viewing unhealthy eating as infrequent, but it wasn't.

Our treat food was a regular part of our diet. Birthday cakes at pre-schools most weeks, sausage sizzles, cake stalls, chocolate fundraisers for schools and sports teams. We were eating like Kings and as if most days are Christmas day. Pies, white bread and fizzy drink were appearing as cheaper options, but the cost on well-being of us and our children was high.

As I explored better ways, it was okay if sometimes they were not quite hitting the mark in taste, I would try again. I heard to give it a go 5 different ways first. Brussel Sprouts roasted and finely sliced finally worked for me. If you or your family members perceive yourselves as fussy eaters, simply try some more. I also find soups another great way to obtain more good nutrition. Smoothies and soups are handy options to get the greens in, or things you, or your kids aren't currently as fussed on, (but know it's good for you).

You can find that healthy tasty way too.

Yoga

Some say that yoga is food for the soul. It's another way of filling up your cup.

You can visualise yourself doing this yoga exercise or do it. Either way is fine. If you don't know how, simply imagine you do, or do an Internet search "sun salutation" yoga poses online. Below are the words that go with the salutation to the sun movements. There are 12 movements, and the 12th is back to the start Mantric Surya Namaskar.

- 1. I hold up my head to face the world. Before I face the world, I must be able to face myself.

- 2. As I stretch. I feel joyous and uplifted.

- 3. As I bow down. I remind myself I may have down moments, during which I learn to rest in my inner being.

- 4. I am ready to run life's race.

- 5. I close my eyes and feel the strength and balance within my being.

- 6. I acknowledge the earth, which is mother to us all.

- 7. My spirit rises from the earth in jubilation.

- 8. I am as high as a mountain. I feel the serenity and strength of the mountain within me.

- 9. I am filled with confidence.

- 10. I turn within and acknowledge my inner being.

- 11. I open my arms, my hands and my heart to the realisation of the beauty and worth of the heavens, the stars and the sun.

- 12. I feel the harmony and peace within me. I am thankful and serene.

Those words have been sitting in my file since 2004, but these practices date back to the ancient yogis. The years come and go and now can be a beautiful time to revisit them, to be put in print and action once more. I thank my yoga teacher and friend Pauline and all the yogis that have been for letting me share a light of yoga here with you too.

6 Cornerstones of Success

The six cornerstones of success are:

1. Successful people want others to succeed rather than others to fail.

2. You are continuously learning instead of thinking you

know it all.

3. You talk about ideas and solutions, rather than talking judgmentally and being critical of other people.

4. You take responsibility, instead of blaming others for their failures.

5. You are forgiving, rather than holding grudges.

6. You are embracing change, instead of afraid of change.

How are your 6 cornerstones? Do you need to fix a few up? As you practice and play with these at another level, you can see how each one benefits you.

Defining Success

What is your personal definition of success?

Starting by documenting it:

Wealth. Accomplishments. Winning.

Be mindful, are you chasing someone else's version of success?

• What is success to you?

• What outcome do you wish to achieve?

• How do you want to feel?

• How do you want them to feel?

Parents of a youngster who has not achieved an A or B may make them feel that they have failed. Judgement in this way, using the grading method isn't so nice, if you're not that A or B student. Webster's dictionaries definition of success was "accumulation of possessions or power and prestige."

A Young & Rubicam's Brand Asset Valuator (BAV) research of consumer habits showed these trends:

Consumers now resist buying brands / products associated with these adjectives:

• Exclusive • Arrogant • Sensuous • Daring

Consumers now prefer these brand images:

• Kindness and empathy • Friendly • High quality • Socially responsible

Never try to be better than someone else, but be the best you can be, that is under your control and the other isn't.

Faith

 You must have faith that things are going to work out as they should. Too often we expect things to work out just the way we want them to.

You and I are the ones who determine our own success. It's up to us. It's what you do and you're never going to fail, if you don't start blaming others for your mistakes. What would it feel like to be your new version of successful?

Make today the best day, do the things that you can control and let others fade away, focusing on doing the best that you can. Do your best, that helps everyone succeed, having masterpiece days and in so having a masterful life.

Let's plant great seeds together and water them well.

If it's to be, perhaps it really is up to you, your attitude affects your altitude. Your mindset success settings are adjusted.

Remember it's all okay. You're in the right place at the right time.

CHAPTER 5: MEDITATION, MINDFULNESS AND SLEEP

"I dwell in possibility." Emily Dickinson

Emily Elizabeth Dickinson (1830-1886) was an American poet.

Meditation and Being Mindful

As we take a deeper look at meditation and mindfulness, past experiences can come to the surface of what worked well and what challenges we may have had.

I remember learning Transcendental Meditation (TM), in the early 1990's. I thought that it would provide the missing link in my development. Here I was using a personalised mantra, to help the mind settle down and transcend beyond normal thought processes, to a state of deep restful alertness. Simple, Natural, Effortless, Easy.

I had read a lot of the research, was already doing yoga, thought I ate well, and regularly exercised. Additionally, I was consuming a lot of high-quality supplements to support my mind and body at that time.

Other people following a similar regime to me, were shouting from the rooftops of their excitement and transformation. I was supposedly doing all the right things, but I wasn't feeling any better, what was I missing? I was being reminded that we are all unique in our results and so many other ways. Sometimes it's also to find out what we don't yet know. These good habits we have can be enhanced further. Things can work out even better. I was also mindful that what could be missing is our link with our true self, tuning in at a deeper level and then noticing more.

School of Life

The action steps I was taking were all great, but they weren't providing me the results I wanted, well not yet anyway. Lucky I was in the school of life and there was more for me to learn and know. I was a willing and curious student with discernment. So, what else did I need to have awareness of, learn and know? Which habits were really the healthiest ones and here to serve me and the planet best?

Sustainability, simplicity and reaching the true heights of our capabilities.

The underlying message: Do no harm; no harm to yourself or others in this process.

Although applying these great habits didn't provide me the expected results, they led me to explore lots of beautiful aspects and really know myself. They made me realise to be more mindful. We are here to learn, understand and experience the fullness of life, which is well beyond us achieving just specific goals.

From the age of 26 - 36, I spent 10 years meditating for 20 minutes, every morning and 20 minutes every night. Never missing a morning or night no matter what was occurring in my outer life.

Initially I did this more formalised meditation known as TM, as a smart proactive tool. This was before meditation in its many forms was popularised as the more mainstream method it is now.

I recall that people thought it a bit weird, or "New Agey," or "Hippyish," back then, so I had to have a strong resolve. Not wanting to be labelled or stereotyped, I used to say I was having a rest. It seemed much easier and acceptable at the time.

Beatles and TM

Before this, in the late 1960's at the height of Beatlemania, the Beatles attended a TM seminar at Bangor Normal College in Wales in August 1967. They were impressed by Maharishi's teachings and decided to study with Maharishi Mahesh Yogi, TM's founder, in India. The Beatles' interest in TM was part of a broader embrace of Indian philosophy and music in their work. John Lennon said that TM was a way to achieve peace of mind and that the phrase "it's gonna be alright," in one of their songs came from something they learned during the course. George Harrison said that TM was a way to connect with God and that it gave him a "buzz" that was better than drugs. The Beatles' music was inspired by their experiences with TM. The Beatles' endorsement of TM helped popularise the technique as an alternative to psychedelic drugs.

What I observed was that interesting judgements were still being made in the 1990's from all that occurred during that time.

More recently Paul McCartney and Ringo Starr performed together for the David Lynch Foundation's "Change Begins Within" charity concert on April 4, 2009. The concert was held at Radio City Music Hall in New York City. The event raised money and awareness for the Foundation's goal to teach one million at-risk children how to meditate.

Better and Better

 Luckily as time passes, we are becoming more accepting and less judgemental as human beings. In writing that statement I am very aware that many may not agree, we human beings haven't done a good job of being accepting and non-judgemental "yet". Yet I live in hope and trust that many of us will and can do better and be better. There's still a bit of work to be done, but we can become better versions of ourselves. Let's cheer each other on and take on the belief that every day and in every way, we are getting better and better and better.

I leaned in, with the knowledge that there would be no harm

to me or others in continuing with this meditation process, perhaps quite the opposite could happen. There could be great benefits for me, my family and humanity.

With the huge volumes of scientific data as validation, I felt grateful. At that time (and even now) we needed the validation. The scientific world was a handy tool and required as proof in our distrusting world. It was used to reduce criticism and scepticism.

I believe we can really tune in to our inner wisdom more. Have this working without having to have as much validation from others. Your actions provide proof of your ability to be wise, trustworthy, centred, intelligent and a great decision maker in life.

I knew that having this practice was beneficial. I also noticed during this time a lot of big life challenges were coming up for me to go through. I was even wondering was this technique working for me? It was a great tool and then I thought, it could become a crutch, and I felt uncertain. The underlying feeling I had was one of "need" and "I have to" do this.

Do you find the terms "need," "must," and "have to" place extra pressure and restrictions on you too?

I decided it was important and healthy to release that need, have to, must, from this as well. I replaced it with "I choose to," and stood in my own power, not only here, but in lots of pressure situations. I can always choose and so can you.

I still choose to and decided that I could still meditate, but more on my own terms. My realisation of the must, need to, have to, do this, was an opportunity to reflect and find a better way and thought process. I stepped back, explored other forms of meditation and mindfulness practices. I asked more questions and had a knowing that I can tune in to the bigger wiser aspects of me, breathe into and live from this awareness and tap into the wisdom of nature too. I continue TM from a choice, get to, perspective and lens. I felt it was a privilege and joy to do, not to be a great meditator, but from it, to have an even better life experience.

The awareness I had intellectually was of the numerous benefits that it provides my mind, body and spirit. The deeper inner peace I was gaining allowed me to respond better to life. The drops of coherence and positivity into the world meant it just felt like the right thing to do for me and humanity.

Technology of Consciousness

I had a practical technology of consciousness where the field of pure intelligence was awakened in the physiology, restoring balance, dissolving stress, and allowing nature's intelligence to flow without restriction. Some of this language I use here may feel foreign and be a bit of a stretch for those who simply want to feel better, sleep better, have more energy and vitality and yes, dissolve stress too, but stick with me and allow this other level of awareness through. There were more than 600 scientific studies over a 35-year period at universities and research institutions around the world. They were documenting the effectiveness of the TM, TM Siddhi and Yogic Flying programmes in promoting physical and mental health, in reversing the aging process, reducing medical care usage and costs, relieving a variety of chronic diseases (including hypertension, heart disease, and asthma), and reducing psychological distress and substance abuse.

What also sparked my interest was the Maharishi Effect and the benefits of Group Practice. This is the phenomenon of 1% of the population practicing the Transcendental Meditation technique improving the quality of life in the larger society. The effect created by a group of the square root of 1% of the population practicing the Transcendental Meditation and TM-Siddhi program including Yogic Flying is called the Extended Maharishi Effect. Research carried out internationally by multiple research teams to investigate the theory and research on the Maharishi

Effect began in the early 1970s and continues to the present day. Of the studies on the Transcendental Meditation and TM-Siddhi program, more than 50 have investigated its effects on society.

The Studies

These studies have shown such changes as reductions in crime, accidents, mortality, war, and terrorism and improvements in economic indicators and the general quality of life. The holistic improvements in society on the scales of entire cities, states, nations, and the world with the predicted outcomes on specific social indicators, were also lodged in advance with independent project review boards. "When the Unified Field of Natural Law becomes lively in the collective consciousness of society, the society functions coherently, social stress dissolves, and the society becomes balanced and healthy."

Having these practices can be so powerful and just like other forms of technology, choose to let it serve you well. I get to, I choose, to and I welcome in the ability to enliven nature's intelligence within the body. As I do this, I am said to be creating ideal states of balance and integration. I continue allowing all that is for my highest good, the highest good of all, and for the highest good of Earth, in the most harmonious coherent ways. I get to meet wonderful people from all sorts of backgrounds and beliefs who practice this technique too.

What if we have enough of us twice daily tapping into the unified field and raising consciousness? If we use these technologies of consciousness in groups around the world we can get to notice and experience firsthand what the research says. What if we get to see humanity uplifted in the process and enjoying highest good. Greek Philosopher Aristotle believed the highest good for humans is eudaimonia, which is often translated as "happiness." He defined eudaimonia as the activity of the soul that is in accordance with virtue or excellence.

There are many great habits to implement on this path, so we do feel better and better.

Useful Habits

Here are some suggestions for practical habits that can be beneficial during this process:

A cornerstone of great MEDS: Meditation, Exercise, Diet, Sleep.

• Tuning into your body so you are eating when it is ready to digest the food.

• Enjoy good fats like Avocados & Walnuts to replace your sugar cravings.

• Cutting out or limiting processed food.

• Closing your kitchen by 7pm.

• Getting morning sunrise sunlight.

• Going for a 20-minute walk before midday.

• Movement, even a little movement is good.

• Implement Strength / Resistance training.

• Performing some form of cardiovascular exercise. This can even be in the form of walking, if done at a speed in which you are increasing your heart rate. Take the stairs, dance, run, cycle; take up a new class or sporting activity.

• Meditation, being in stillness, allowing thought to come and go and opening the portals beyond this thinking mind. Exploring 20 minutes twice a day or TM. Alternatively put aside 3 minutes, 3 times a day as there are proven benefits of even doing this small amount.

• Mindfulness, focusing one's awareness on the present moment, while calmly acknowledging and accepting one's feelings, thoughts, and bodily sensations.

Most people can carry out many, or all these habits. It may seem daunting or too challenging at first, but as a line from the poem,

The Mountain by Laura Ding-Edwards says, "If the mountain seems too big today then climb a hill instead." If you have any doubts of your capabilities, check in with your chosen experts.

Observations

Within all of this, open to you and what is uniquely right for you.

What you can do to determine what's right for you:

• Observe how you feel.

• Observe what you are resisting.

• Observe what you are saying yes to, but really want to say no.

• Observe what you are saying no to, but a yes is what you really wanted to say.

You're requiring your own stretch right now, so let's tap into your body and shift some energy there too. Release anything that's a bit stagnant.

Based on my research and current understandings I see meditation as a fundamental part of a holistic package. It is a great base and has a big impact. A practice that provides beautiful pillars to support your mind, body and spirit.

I am also mindful of stress being the common risk factor of 75%-90% of diseases, including the diseases which cause the foremost morbidity and mortality. As over 600 studies attest to the effectiveness of TM, it's worth exploring and finding out for yourself. They have free online introductory talks as well.

The realisation from this is that there is no one magic bullet to reach your nirvana, enlightenment, or awakening. It may not even follow a linear progression. A package of good habits including a meditation practice where you transcend can be a smart way forward.

As you step out it can be a bit cloudy at times. The clouds are in front of the sun. This doesn't diminish its strength, power and value. It shines brightly despite the clouds. The sun is content to be behind the scenes sometimes. Whether the sun is shining bright or lining the clouds with a golden hue, it is valuable. Keeping up that which serves you well, can have you shining like the sun in your own way. That you are here now means you are strong, powerful and valued too.

Moving Forward

You press pause on your busy mind, all those meanings you were giving to situations that were causing you stress or pain. You move through them into stillness. You are the observer and witness with a higher better view.

Notice what is, or could be your experience:

• Have you found you handle your life better with meditation, such as feeling more relaxed, less stressed and not so negative?

• What if you are choosing to live a life in meditation? You are aware and witnessing yourself as you are living your life, present, alert, peaceful, elated.

• You could be choosing to live an elevated existence.

It wouldn't seem right to talk about this without giving you more of your own personal experience. A behind the scenes little tour, the how to.

Mindfulness

Practicing Mindfulness involves focusing on the present moment without judgement.

- Be an impartial witness of your own experience.
- Accept the present moment.
- Have a beginner's mind, open and curious to new experiences.
- Trust yourself and your feelings.
- Let go of judgements and thoughts that aren't serving

you.

Tune into your body, do a body scan noticing sensations.

- Mindful eating, engaging your senses appreciating the food you are eating.
- Mindful listening, giving your full attention to what someone is sharing with you.
- Mindful breathing using breathing techniques to relax your body and mind.
- Guided imagery to relax your body and mind.

Here are some Meditation options:

- Guided Meditations

- Mindfulness Meditation

- Body Scan Meditation

- Loving Kindness Meditation

- Transcendental Meditation

- Walking and Breathing Meditations

- Yoga and Qi Gong

How to Meditate: Accepting the challenge, learn to meditate. Ideally, check out the Free Introductory Talks that I mentioned (see resources for links) to explore and see if that feels a fit.

There are many powerful breathing practices. One that I do which you can utilise too is, Pranayama Breathing (alternate nostril breathing). This as well as Yoga Asanas (exercises) both complement and enhance your meditation practice.

The OMT: One Minute Technique

Take this minute in a safe space. Ideally this space is where you will not be disturbed. If in company you can simply say, "give me a minute."

• Sit in a comfortable upright position with hands in your lap or standing with hands relaxed by your side.

• Your feet flat on the floor, shoulders and jaw relaxed.

• Put your timer on for 1 minute.

• With your eyes closed or looking downward, count your breath on each exhale.

• Notice your breath.

• At the end note which number you reached.

• Notice the relaxed feeling you now have.

Tuning In

The tuning into your body can also be done with pulse diagnosis; this was used in Ayurveda, traditional Chinese medicine and others. It was often referred to as a diagnostic technique like the "MRI" of traditional medical systems. Through the rhythms of your pulse, feeling at your wrist, you can feel and get to know the three different pulses. Also, through pulse diagnosis, a physician can identify the physiological imbalances at the basis of disease. It's effective at identifying the root cause of the disease and most effective treatment. It aids prevention and identifying imbalances at early stages when it's easier to correct and before the imbalance manifests as a clinical disease.

Feeling

Rhythms of Your Pulse

If you're wearing a watch remove this, so you can feel the different pulses. As a female place your right hand around your left wrist, your three middle fingers coming over the top and feeling downward. Inside the top part of your inside wrist, feel the pulse of your Dosha's: Vata, Pitta, and Kapha.

For a male you do the same process but place your left hand around your right wrist.

Pulse Diagnosis Diagram, where to feel on your wrist.

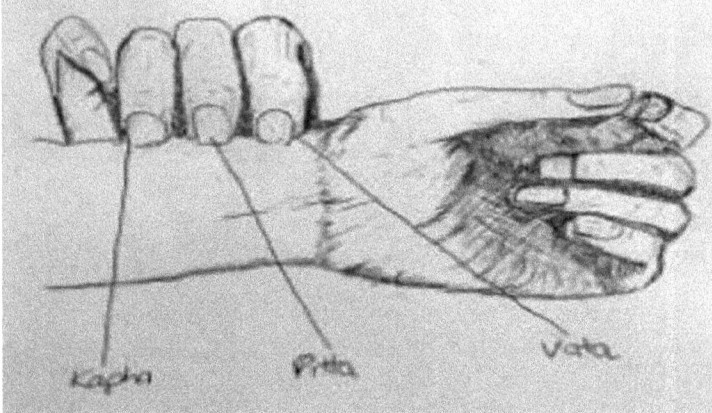

In that touch and awareness, feel the pulses. Notice each one and their different rhythm and beat. Then notice them settle and balance. You are beginning the process of balancing your body in this simple act.

Getting Clear

Get really clear about what you do want to achieve and enjoy. How necessary is it for you to be performing at your best in this situation?

Who needs you to show up and serve with strength and excellence?

Why is it important to grow right now at this point of your life?

It's never too late to start your best life ever - now.

Sleep

When you review these success settings, sleep has been one that many grapple with. Is your intention to enjoy a deep rejuvenating sleep each night?

Sleep, restful rejuvenating sleep how do you achieve this?

Experts suggest that extra sleep (that magical 8 hours) will improve your cognitive scores by 22% within 7 days.

8 Top Sleep Tips

Here are 8 top tips for you to achieve a great sleep. The other success settings of yoga, meditation, exercise, food and drink are all included and have influence here too.

1. Caffeine. This can be a no brainer for many to cut the tea or coffee habit before bed. Be mindful that some of your favourite herbal teas, drinks and even flavoured water have caffeine. Ones that boast energy-boosting benefits are likely culprits.

Stop sipping these from 2pm experts suggest. If you enjoy a wine, let's say 6pm rather than 11pm. As for the herbal tea, it can be a calming one in the evening such as Fennel, Chamomile or Lavender. Hot water and a couple of slices of ginger is my drink of the day suggestion. Ginger has calmative and alkalising properties too.

2. Naps. Avoid naps in the afternoon, if you must power nap during the day, try a 20-minute meditation instead.

3. Darkness and light. Set the mood with low lighting. Dimness signals the biological clock that it's time to wind down, while bright light says "daytime." Keeping your room dark and free from noise and other distractions while you sleep.

Consider blackout curtains, eye shades, ear plugs. The "white noise" could be in the form of machines, humidifiers, fans and other devices. Expose yourself to sunlight in the morning. This will keep your circadian rhythms in check.

4. Evaluate the rest of your room. Do you have a comfortable mattress and pillows?

5. Big or spicy meals can cause discomfort from indigestion. If you can, avoid large meals for two to three hours before bedtime.

Did you know that a light whole-wheat pasta dish with fresh vegetables, a little diced chicken breast, tomato sauce, and a sprinkle of Parmesan contain a snooze friendly combination of protein, and tryptophan, an amino acid that converts to sleep promoting serotonin in the body. A small bowl of cottage cheese with banana slices is another dish that serves up tryptophan. If you are eating a wholefoods plant-based diet, nuts and seeds like pumpkin seeds, sunflower seeds, almonds along with legumes like beans, lentils and chickpeas are all good sources of protein and tryptophan.

6. Relaxing bedtime rituals. Be consistent with bedtime and wake up time. Having a bath as a ritual, yes, but not right before turning in. Anything that raises your body temperature too close to bedtime may hinder you from falling asleep. The ideal room temperature is reported to be 15.5 - 19.4 degrees Celsius.

7. Exercise daily. Gentle restorative yoga can help put your mind at ease, steady your breath and reduce muscle tension without revving up your heart.

Yoga pose: Lie on your back with the soles of your feet together and your knees bent and dropping toward the floor. Place your arms, palms up, by your sides, keeping your shoulders back and your chest open. Close your eyes and inhale through your nose while slowly counting to four, then exhale while counting back down to one. Continue for 10 minutes, or as long as it takes you to feel fully relaxed.

8. Disconnect an hour before bed. No sending of that email or text just before you turn in. Unplug, turn your phone off as it's possible that even the vibration could disturb sleep if a person is cued to hear or respond to.

Too much time on electronic devices in the evening can have us too wired as well. Computers, phones and TV's can affect our sleep. Consensus from studies is that the blue light that LED screens give off can slow or halt the production of melatonin.

Melatonin is the hormone that signals our brain that it's time for bed.

Listen to Your Body

I find our minds can be wired some nights, so we really need to start that wind down earlier. Write it out and relieve your mind. The writing it out is best done earlier in the evening perhaps 6pm or 7pm. The outcome you're trying to achieve is relaxation and a release of the day's events.

What to Write:

The subjects that you can write about could include:

- What's gone well?
- What you want to do better?
- Notes of what's on your agenda for tomorrow.
- What you are grateful for.

The reason for this is to release the tendency of thinking your way through things, when it is time to sleep.

Your thoughts can keep you busy, and you may think this is a good time to reflect, but not if it's keeping you awake at night.

You've written down whatever you need to and anything else can be handed over, to the universe, or your greater self.

A statement you can repeat is:

• "Whatever I need to know, remember, do, I will, thank you. I now release and surrender this, and I am grateful for a wonderful rejuvenating sleep." "Good night."

Extra Sleep Tips

Another tool I use from my restful sleep toolbox.

Sneak in a "tighten and release" of your body. This is also known as progressive muscle relaxation, where you tighten or tense muscle groups in your body, then release the tension.

After doing this process, count down from 100 - 0 with slow belly breathing saying the word "deeper" in your mind with each number as you count down. Repeat this process of counting down until you fall asleep.

Want to go further?

Of course, there are more tips and details as we continue our mastery.

One of my clients found understanding the sleep cycle helpful as well. They were then more relaxed and accepting as they knew having lighter patches was part of a normal sleep pattern.

N1 NREM non rapid eye movement, also known as light sleep,

N2 the second stage of NREM sleep,

N3 the third stage of NREM sleep,

and REM the fourth stage of sleep when you dream.

Most people go through 4-6 sleep cycles per night. A typical sleep cycle lasts 90-110 minutes. The first cycle is shorter while later cycles are longer. REM sleep increases as the night progresses.

A sleep diary can be great to help you better evaluate common patterns, or issues you may see with your sleep, or sleeping habits. Check in with your chosen expert if you are after more assistance.

• What sort of possibility are you choosing to dwell and be in?

Remember it's all okay. You're in the right place at the right time.

CHAPTER 6: EXPERIENCING THE SHIFT

"Feelings are much like waves; we can't stop them from coming, but we can choose which one to surf." Jonatan Martensson

Numerous researchers have found smiling makes us feel happier and can help to lift the sense of sadness being experienced.

Exercising Your Smile Muscles

This is exciting for us as we have a muscle, lots of them in fact, both mentally and physically, so for them to be strong and agile, requires practice, and you can do this. By the way you have 43 muscles in your face alone.

If you look at your face, and you don't like what you see, what are you to do? Do you want to experience a shift? It may not be a face lift that some feel they need, but it can help your sense of wellbeing.

The test subjects who were required to smile compared to those who weren't, reported feeling happier than the non-grinners. They knew they were acting, but their bodies didn't and so their bodies responded accordingly.

Positivity

With your willingness, the positive ripple effect can occur and has the ability to positively uplift many. Let's smile, lifting each other up one person at a time.

You never know what's going on in people's lives, so showing patience and compassion are always good default settings to have for others. Have this for yourself too. It's important to keep your cup of well-being full and overflowing, especially if you want to offer and give more.

Sometimes as we move forward things don't happen straight away. To experience the shift we must persevere. We might try things once, twice, six times even, until eventually maybe the 12th time we nail it. Most people give in well before this breakthrough. Do remember if you are continuing forward, practice does not make perfect, but "perfect practice" makes perfect.

Take a golfer who keeps practicing and has an error in his golf swing. If he continues without instruction all he's doing is practicing his error.

A lovely gentleman had a successful career and was facing a few speed bumps. His job came to an end, and he had quite a few months without work. He's a smart, capable guy and is going to find something great. Eventually he did. He did have low moments and didn't think it would take this long or be quite this difficult. Deep down however he knew it would all work out and continued upskilling, studying, looking and learning.

On this day he was leaving a parking building as another lady entered, he simply gave his ticket to her, it was valid for the rest of the day. A simple and nice gesture that made that ladies day, and in so doing uplifted him as well. He wasn't focusing on himself but seeing how he could assist and show kindness to another.

What would our world look like if we all did one kind act for another every day?

What you have observed in our current world shift is that there has been some discord to face. This can occur initially and just like that gentleman experienced, these changes and transitions can last longer than we would wish. It's not necessarily a comfortable zone for anyone and there can be conflicts, disharmony and division. When you look broader you may notice some political craziness has already occurred. When you look to the stars there are some planetary shifts. When you look around there has been much uneasiness and concern, but when you look within, you may find an anchor of peace to help you through.

Your Focus

Winston Churchill gave his famous "Never give in" speech, Sia has a song "Never Give up."

Winston Churchill (1874-1965) was an inspirational statesman, writer, orator and leader who led Britain to victory in the Second World War. He served as Conservative Prime Minister twice - from 1940 to 1945 and from 1951 to 1955. (British) Bulldog was the nickname first given to him by the Russians. It was a reference to his ferocity and focus. He was also awarded the Nobel Prize in Literature in 1953.

One of Winston Churchill's famous speeches was "Never Give In." This was delivered at Harrow School on October 29, 1941. In his address, Churchill urged people to "never give in, except to convictions of honour and good sense." The speech was given during World War II, when the United Kingdom was fighting against Nazi Germany.

Sia Kate Isobelle Furler is an Australian singer and songwriter. Born and raised in Adelaide, she started her career as a singer in the acid jazz band Crisp in the mid-1990s. When Crisp disbanded in 1997, she released her debut studio album, OnlySee, in Australia.

Focusing

Throughout it all you can still stay centred, strong and clear. It starts with you. Look for and see the true loving better brighter side of humanity and let the loving light in you shine through. Be very mindful of this and the space you choose to be.

What do you want to give your attention to and create more of?

Some great people can accidentally get caught up and focus on the lack, fear, perceived dangers and inadvertently create more of that which they do not want. Instead, you can start asking for and choosing the centred calm peaceful solution space and state of being. Make a commitment to do this for the next month and let me know what shows up for you. Hopefully you will keep doing this forever.

If there's enough of a shift in your own mindset, you will see that there is more of the light than the darkness on the planet right now. You may notice that some of these dark patches are noisy and get highlighted, through your media and news. Use these observations as a highlight of a shift, a pivot, an opening for something good to enter and keep being part of that light and goodness yourself.

Life is a bigger version of you, so the same things you use to improve yourself also improve our planet. The phrases "you are made of stardust" and "your energy matters" hold many truths. You do make a difference, perhaps a lot more than you've ever realised before. Explore these truths. Science, the ancient Greeks, and the ancient Rishis in India accepted that the Universe, including you, is made of energy, not matter. Newtonian physics moved onto Quantum physics. We are all created of atomic energy waves.

The ancient Greeks lived in mainland Greece, the Greek Islands, and in colonies around the Mediterranean Sea. They were famous for their contributions to philosophy, astronomy, science, medicine, physics, mathematics, art, and culture. They also invented democracy and the Olympic games.

The ancient Rishis of India were revered sages and seers who used meditation to gain insight and create knowledge. They contributed to India's spiritual and philosophical heritage. As wise teachers they were also associated with sacred rituals and hymns.

Letting Go

What if you are here to open to the goodness that is in you and in us all. What if you are here to not only radiate more of that, but to be the embodiment of love, which is goodness. What if you are here to do your thing by following your passions in the best ways you can. To do this you are letting go of the old ways of being and believing that is limiting. Systems that hold you in fear, old stories of not being good enough. Step into more that serves the happier, healthier, more powerful vibrant you. Hold this better vision you now have of yourself or know could be possible. Do the actions that support its creation.

Our lives have been full of communications and contrasts. The waves of the ocean come and go, just like your thoughts, feelings and emotions. As a human you can have a habit of a negative bias, and getting stuck, often in your fears, worries and regrets. You can accidentally be in your own way. The good news is that there is no time like the present to practice making the shift and creating some new habits. These are for the next best version of who you really are and can be.

Behind the Scenes

Another day is unfolding, and I am about to go on a call, one of my mastermind calls. What tools are you utilising in your tool kit, what masterminds are you bringing together?

To embrace all that is and experience a shift into a new level of clarity and enjoyment you hear and respect other perspectives and stretch yourself beyond your current understanding. On such calls, you are supported and lovingly challenged as needed. A reflection of what others heard you say, and inspired thought comes back to you. You listen, reflect and share other perspectives and inspired ideas too.

You achieve another level of awareness and step forward into more service from a space of love and loving kindness, integrity, growth and action.

When you are experiencing shifts, you can experience love and delight, fear and doubt. The opposite to love is fear. Fear had what could be described as a debilitating effect on us.

I used to interpret FEAR as "**F**alse **E**vidence **A**ppearing **R**eal." There is a new meaning you can also use to serve you in fear.

FEAR: The New Meaning

 Face **E**verything **A**nd **R**ise.

May you implement this new meaning and feel excited and empowered as you track your small daily wins utilising this skill.

Thank you to the beautiful Angie Johnsey for your sharing of this new meaning to choose for fear. Angie is a gorgeous heart centred creator, here to shed more love in the world and raise the level of consciousness too. Angie is a mind/mindfulness coach teaching the tools for mindful and healthy relationships with self, others, and life. Teaching you how to feel free from within. Why we must fall in order to rise.

I used the phrase "**F**ace **E**verything **A**nd **R**ise" with a photo of the Washington Monument in one of my social media posts. It was standing tall and piercing through the blue sky glistening in the sun. You can also stand tall, bright and strong in the face of any fear.

Telomeres

 As you go inward you have your wisdom tool kit to draw on and your body has trillions of cells. An essential part of human cells are your telomeres, these affect how your cells age. Telomeres are the caps at the end of each strand of DNA that protect your chromosomes, like the plastic tips at the end of shoelaces. Telomere shortening is involved in all aspects of the aging process on a cellular level. They can lengthen too, something that was never thought possible until these last few years.

There's lots of ways to lengthen them and slowing aging throughout this book. To experience the shift and lengthen them here are key elements for you:

- Control and reduce stress.

- Exercise regularly.

- Eat a range of food for antioxidant and vitamin benefits.

- Practice meditation and yoga.

Many of the tips and tools to execute this are within these pages too. You don't need to feel "pressured" to do all these immediately, but to truly "grow" you may want to begin with at least one of them or improve and enhance another.

Moving to Your Next Level of Growth and Enjoyment

Here are 5 magical areas for you to explore:

1. Clarity: What if that feels unclear for you, start with being curious and observe your activities you do, what lights you up and what darkens your mood. Observe and write down daily for a week and you'll see some patterns emerging. If there's too much that you don't really love, or like that much, think about trying some new ways. Perhaps what is opposite to those things you disliked could provide you with clarity on what you do like? Find some relief.

Also think back to your childhood, at around ages 8-10, what did you love doing then? What if you're thinking gosh no prospects with my pastimes. I was playing with a Barbie doll, board games, hide and seek, climbing trees and watching TV. Just start playing in the zone of things that make you smile.

Write down any inspired ideas that come to you whilst you're in this zone. Pen and paper are your friend. Regardless how ridiculous the idea may initially seem, no judgement, write it down too. Simply enjoy and see what comes to and through you, or even who, or what shows up.

If at this stage you have any repetitive negative talk coming up, grab a pencil. I heard that using graphite takes the thoughts from you and to the paper. Write them down, e.g. sadness, anger, frustration, forgiveness, whatever comes up, write the words down and then light a match to them. This might take a few matches, so do it in a safe place, where you are not lighting anything else, perhaps within the confines of a special bowl?

The ashes that are left, you can now blow them to the wind. If some words stay, note what they are and burn again. Those words that were the hardest to burn are perhaps the trickiest things for you to let go of.

2. Develop the skills. Have the learning mindset that "If you learn these skills or achieve these outcomes, then you'll be in a position to have greater freedom and choice."

• What skills are you developing right now?

Develop the skills you need to reach the next level. I've observed sometimes people are too busy getting the skills for the next level they have forgotten or overlooked the importance of getting the competency where they are at. Be good at what you are already doing, whilst also working at gaining the next level of achievement. This could mean the roles you play in life, as a partner, parent, child, friend, leader, employee, role model.

This is an important ingredient in the secret sauce.

• "Be here now."

It's not so secret; all this information is available to you anytime in the field of possibility.

What many of us are here to do is be in service to humanity. Caring for ourselves and our fellow human beings, letting more goodness in. Actions rooted in kindness and compassion for the betterment of society. Whatever rung on the rail you are at, you can go up to the next even easier.

Skill Development

Don't feel pressured, instead know, that when something is important for you to do, you can up skill if needed and go do it. Or think laterally, how else can I be involved? You'll have varying levels of strength, experience, skills and knowledge. Age does not come into this. There are some very wise souls at 7 years of age, "wise beyond their years" appearing to have a level of understanding or insight that seems unusual for their age. Watch this next generation of babies that are being born into this world now and notice how wise many already are and can be.

We have social conditioning where we are taught to behave and accept certain ways. We can be aware of this and explore what else can be.

Following Your Passions

What if you have a condition that rules you out from doing something that you are passionate about?

This does not mean you cannot follow your passions. You can still be involved in a sport you love as this next gentleman did. He was faced with health challenges that forced him to hang up his boots. His role was not to be as a player in that game. Regardless of how much he tried and even visualised that possibility, it wasn't to be. Instead, he worked towards achieving other skills and abilities. His determination, perseverance, study and willingness meant he undertook the roles of a referee, a coach and an analyst. He allowed this and something even better to come into his life. He didn't give up on his dreams, and he found a new way to deliver in that sport.

Sometimes you've just gotta get out of your own way and let other possibilities in.

3. Infuse old wisdom. Infuse old wisdom, thousands of years old with more recent insights and inspiring knowledge from the last 50 years and present day. Keep asking, keep seeking your clarity. Your job is to make the good even better, and know it is possible. Remember Impossible = I'm possible.

Where to focus?

Sometimes people quit a certain aspect, because it's not having the outcome or progress, they would like or envision. If it is a tool or an activity that you know can get great results you need to speak directly to those who are having great results with it and find out what they are doing.

Having and developing good relationships wherever you go, leaves a line of goodness and positive possibility. You don't need the in-depth detail at this stage; just understand their thinking process, their activity, what they do.

4. Focus. Focus on how you show up, more than speed. Each day show up as your best self, open, engaged and enthusiastic. You'll feel better with your own company and others will enjoy it more too. Let's be interested and excited about life. You achieve faster with full awareness, positive presence and attitude.

5. Decide. Decide: Am I willing to do that? Are you willing to make that much of a commitment, do that much activity, and handle the challenges you may face? Sometimes it simply will not be a fit for you regardless how glamorous and fantastic their results have been. Check in that you are not trying to avoid something. What is your real dream or desire now?

Keep seeking to give and be your best wherever you are. Now choose powerfully, as if everything is on your side.

If you knew everything and everyone was on your side cheering you on, what would you do?

A lady had written a book, she wanted it to be a screenplay and a movie. She thought it was an impossible dream. "Why," said the interviewer, "I go see movies all the time, that's not impossible."

He then got her talking about the dream, who she would have in the movie, which parts and the conversation continued. The only thing impossible was that one of the actors she'd initially chosen was dead. That's okay, choose another actor for that role, and she did.

What is your impossible dream? Perhaps it too is now possible.

Yes

Yes, let's do this:

A. Let's plan to overcome these perceived obstacles, and yes, I'm up for it. Identify what skills you need, become competent in them and enjoy more confidence in the process.

B. Yes it makes good financial and business sense to employ someone to do these aspects for me rather than me managing it all.

No

No, I choose to do something else that is more suited to me; that I will bring out more of my passion and joy with. If you are choosing a no ensure it is from a place of power and possibility, not fear of your current ability.

Questions

• What are your passions and what does bring you great joy and satisfaction?

• How can you incorporate more of this in your work and daily life?

A pros and cons, likes and dislikes, current strengths and lesser strengths list is good to reflect upon.

Remind yourself of what you like, what you're good at and what else you could possibly do. Let's keep thinking outside the box. You do not stop from fear, or stories you've had replayed in your mind. The past experiences were without the knowledge, awareness and foresight you have now. Be clear and honest with yourself. Was this a heck yes, let's do this, or a heck no?

A little bit of nervousness or trepidation can be in there with your "heck yes." You're looking for that initial feeling, before you suppress your excitement.

Both Celine Dion and Bruce Springsteen have been on stage for decades and continue singing to huge crowds at sold out arenas worldwide. Both experience stage fright and are nervous before every show. Your nervousness need not stop you from living out your heart's desires. Turn it into courageousness. Give yourself a deadline. Learn your craft. Involve others, and as the Nike advertisement would say, "Just do it!" Enjoy the process of learning and growing. Don't be afraid to enrol mentors and teachers along the way. No matter what age you are 19 or 99, you can be a lifelong learner too.

Focus, minimise, scale back and quit everything that is not moving you forward. Get out of toxic environments. The story goes that if you don't clear debris and distractions from your life, the universe can't recognise the white space available for something better.

The above guidelines can work very well for those people who are people pleasers and find it hard to say no. If you see yourself with the tendency of "FOMO" - "fear of missing out," or another acronym I like to use "JOMO" - "joy of missing out," implementing such healthy boundaries is empowering.

What if you're a person who says no too often?

The same formula can be used, for clearing these distractions that are holding you back.

The 5-Step Formula

Step 1. Head outside your normal life, changing those habits that may not be so healthy and stretch your comfort zone.

Step 2. Take the challenge and call to adventure. At least once a week try something new, to see how you like it, and say yes. Try something of interest to you, give it a go.

Step 3. Face the refusal and resistance of the change and internal transformation this adventure will bring. You may not love it first time and not want to do it, but also you can warm to the idea and the experience. This may be the next time or the next, maybe you might find you start loving aspects of it. Whatever way you feel, remember you are going outside your safety zone, so it may feel exciting and scary all at once?

Step 4. For some this is uncharted territory, and others a nudge to get back on track. I acknowledge and congratulate you for the journey you are on. You are now meeting the mentor, and being guided by a mentor who provides wisdom, support and help. (Yes, you can take inspiration from this book).

Step 5. The reward, earning a reward for overcoming your greatest fear, weathering a crisis well, greater knowledge and insight. The power of stepping into the unknown, letting go of the familiar.

You are taking your "hero's journey." Movies depict this too, Lion King, Harry Potter, Spiderman, Star Wars, The Matrix, The Hobbit, Finding Nemo. Generally, in these movies the heroes must eventually leave the village or the castle to come into their full powers.

In life we are faced with constant change. Many people are going outside their comfort zones; however, it may have been by default, reacting to situations, because they must. This time you're in the driver's seat and it's because you choose to, it's by design. You are breaking the cycle. You are the movie director and actor in your own scene and film.

Exploring, adventuring into things that you may quite like. On the way you might be surprised to find new things that now appeal. You can be more amazing than you give yourself credit for. If you find you are good at giving yourself credit, how about you share the love. Look around you and give someone else credit too, and maybe even make their day.

Mastery

Determination and extraordinary high vibe energy with such resolve confidence and belief, they're some of the things I like about Brendon Burchard.

I find his work great. He cuts it down to practical bite size pieces and has an ability to inspire people into action. I smile as I recognise so many of these things he shares from my years of study in this field. Brendon offers another level of insight and research, he teaches and trains millions worldwide including the highest achievers that walk this present-day earth, particularly those in sport and business.

The message from him is that if you master these 6 things:

1. Your Physical Energy

2. Mental Energy

3. Spiritual Energy.

4. Your Focus

5. Your Habits

6. And your Willingness to Continually Learn, do and be Better.

The world and you are the greater for it.

Do you notice yourself moving into the fields of limitless possibilities? You can play in these fields more. These fields can include science, nature, spirituality, maths, music and quantum physics. You can even be ready for quantum leaps in your game called life.

You can experience your shift and choose which feelings you want to surf.

Remember it's all okay. You're in the right place at the right time.

CHAPTER 7: TACKLING DEATH

"Let yourself be silently drawn by the strange pull of what you really love. It will not lead you astray." Rumi

Jalal al-Din Muhammad Rumi, Rumi (1207-1273) was a great Sufi mystic, 13th-century poet and Islamic scholar. Rumi's poetry often touches on themes of overcoming fear and persevering through challenges. He often speaks of embracing challenges, finding strength in vulnerability, and using adversity to grow and evolve. In one of his poems, he writes, "Be grateful for whatever comes."

I am lucky, blessed and grateful to be alive and sharing with you now after my own personal shave with death when I was 16 years old.

The year before, as a 15-year-old, I had competed in a Women's triathlon. Luckily, I had entered this as a team event with two friends, one a brilliant swimmer, the other a brilliant runner. My role was the cycling section. We finished in the top 10, and it felt great. The following year I was competing as an individual. In the mornings I was training early at the pool. Swimming was not a strength of mine, and my breathing in freestyle, was more like holding my breath most of the way.

One of these mornings I sunk to the bottom of the pool and had to be rescued and resuscitated. I had no recall of the events; I woke up in hospital, my parents at my side, grateful I was alive.

The years that passed have had repercussions from that day. A lot of learning and relearning was required to enhance my mind, memory, neurological pathways, body and spirit. The healthier I could become in all these areas, the better chances I had of no further issues, or recurrences.

Beginning Again

You may have faced more than your fair share of heartache, tragedy and despair, your trust muscle and even your heart may have felt broken.

I am so sorry and acknowledge your strength, your courage and the pain you have held. I wish for you to allow loving kindness in and release yourself of the heavy burden that suffering can cause. May you find peace and a letting go of any trauma from the events that lead you to this point. Reach out, there is help and support for you no matter where in the world you live.

Beginning your new story. This narrative is the one of victory. This is where we are no longer held captive as victims of the past. Victory is freedom, a successful outcome of a struggle. To inspire you forward you may reflect on how far you have come already. For starters you've made it through childhood, adolescence, and you have made it here, to be reading or hearing this now!

I also found my mum to be a living miracle as she has faced so many life and death challenges. Her deep faith, love of her family and a deep desire to see her children and grandchildren grow kept her going no matter what she faced. We were all so important to her and she always told us that's what kept her alive. Family - Us and her deep faith were her guiding lights.

When I was a young child, I used to speak with my grandmother about death. I was really scared of it, and she helped me feel okay. I later read books about death. I felt the more I knew, the less I would fear. One such book was *Deathing* by Anya Foos-Graber. Elisabeth Kübler-Ross is another writer in this field. I knew the fear of something can be far greater than facing that fear. I could never quite pin down my own belief systems and understanding. Parts of what I read and learnt felt good, but other parts didn't seem to be right in many cases.

There are so many ways and circumstances in which we lose our loved ones.

I recall a story of us being like leaves on a tree, the young leaves fall as well as the old. This was about us not knowing what age someone will pass. They could be young or old. It can happen at any length and stage of life. Some passings are sudden, others slow, some are feeling ready to go, others not so. It could be an accident, a medical event, an act of war or terrorism, a suicide, an assisted death, a natural disaster, it could be at work, at home, or when out and about, at night or during the day.

None of this was to create a fear of dying at any time, but rather the universality of it all. No matter who or where we are, we are all affected and face loss. With this awareness we get to understand the preciousness of life. We have an opportunity to strengthen our ability to make the most of being here now and dealing with loss.

Even though we are talking about death, grief can be the death of a pet, or loss such as an ending of a relationship, retirement, pregnancy, financial state, work. Grief is caused by the end of, or change in a familiar pattern of behaviour, the conflicting feelings.

As we acknowledge the ways we exit our physical bodies it is with respect we honour one another and the journey we are each on. Blessings and Healing prayers to you for everything you've had to face and all the feelings and emotions that arise. May you find solace here too.

My Dad

I knew theoretically the belief systems and patterns and the ability to bounce forward better than before, but could I do it when it came my turn to face my dad's death?

During the writing of this book my dad passed and here is a little piece of how I felt:

Yesterday afternoon I felt much sadness and tears as I faced the news of my dad's struggle. He is fighting to survive now and taking one day at a time. I feel so grateful that I'm able to not tear up as I write this, which is quite beautiful and remarkable. The main reason for that is Dad does not feel that it is his time just yet and he still wants to live here on this planet with us. With that in mind I'm fully supportive of seeing him as well and vibrant as he can be. I feel proud and honoured that I can feel strong and be sending love and strength to him and others in the universe who need it at this time too. (Perhaps that's all of us?) It didn't feel right for me to go with a story that my father wasn't seeing as his current truth. Why create sadness in my life when it doesn't have to be there at this moment, nor send a vibration out of more sorrow.

During this time, I was very mindful of how our minds create the stories we tell, and our bodies follow the cues. I was aware of my thoughts and emotions. The interpretations of our world stem from these stories as we try to make sense of things. This can have us seeing situations in a skewed way, not always objective and not all of it true. The point of awareness being we don't have to believe everything our minds tell us. Our thoughts can be influenced by biases, emotions, and past experiences, often leading to inaccurate interpretations of reality. I knew how important it is to critically evaluate and analyse thoughts, question the logic, consider different perspectives and verify information before accepting it as true.

What this meant was I hadn't told too many people about how truly tricky it is for Dad right now. He had less than 10% heart function for the last 4 years, and now things were looking worse. I didn't want the energy of giving up on him to be the energy to take through. My experience was that too many people had people dead and buried, written them off, when they heard more. I came from a family of strong determined people who didn't fall at the first hurdle but courageously carried on and proved people wrong. If it felt beneficial for me to share, then I would. What I do know is "if we believe we can handle whatever comes our way, and that it is a gift into a more beautiful expression" - we can, we do, so it is and can be.

Diagnosis and Prognosis

You do not have to fit into outside predictions of your fate. Yes, sometimes my dad was considered to be just surviving. At other times he was happy, excited and having a good laugh. He wouldn't miss this crazy human journey, even with all its pitfalls, there were great times too. He was here no matter what the Dr's said. He found his own way through. He was aware of his limitations but also knew that he can do this and be "okay." He could have a decent amount of quality in his life still. Yes, it was tough at times, but he chose to live and thrive whenever he could.

These words I've written and my raw emotion that is coming through are as a reminder to us, that we can navigate these caverns and dark periods well if we find ourselves in them. We can find the light, flow and still be okay. We may deal with grief in different stages, order and time frames, there is no normal way. Feelings and stages we experience can be denial, anger, bargaining, hopelessness and acceptance.

I had gone to the deepest level of understanding that I could and was accepting and trusting that Dad would leave his earthly body when the time was right for him. Dad passed on Mother's Day morning. We were there with him. We saw him take his last breath. He was now at peace. My dad had left his earthly body.

I chose to use this hurt I felt to strengthen my own spirit and love of life. I knew Dad would want that too. There was no pressure on me to do anything but what I felt was right for me. I was not bypassing anything but feeling it all. Dad wanted us to get on with our lives, and we all would in our own right ways and times. Our ability to handle the hurts and see them as a life lesson for us to learn and grow from is a powerful reminder also.

Does this mean I do not cry, or I do not anger. I'd like to think I anger less and am able to quickly go to a space of neutrality. Here you do not get too entangled and can take a step back from the situation and into gratitude. The tears, well they still happen, you are not here to "not" express your emotions but find good ways of expression that serve you and others. If tears are to flow, you can allow that as well.

Powerful tools are available for us. Helplines are available if you need them too. Something that came through strongly for me when Dad passed is present mind awareness. What I would do is notice when my mind started going towards things, thoughts, feelings that didn't serve me, that created more of what didn't make me feel so good. I would do a shift, mental, or physical, or both.

My Mum

It is 23rd January 2025. I felt drawn to do some edits and additions to this book. There's a lot that has happened in these last 7 years, much of which I will not speak of in this edition. The guiding principles that are here are timeless. With life's twists and turns, we can still have an anchor of inner peace.

In three days, on the 26th of January, it will be the 1st anniversary of my mum's passing. Mum knew it was her time. Life had become too much of a struggle. She said she didn't have any fight left in her. We didn't want her to have to be trying and fighting. Giving of her best was always enough. We loved her and she always knew that. Mum was inspiring to so many and in so many ways. When you talk of never giving up, or giving in, handling life with grace, being a loving beautiful human no matter what life hands you - She was that and more.

Having been in and out of hospital like a yo-yo, each time harder to bounce back and move forward, than before, she had now reached the end. She was at peace with dying and ready for the transition. Twenty-six years had passed since her first cancer diagnosis, the struggles she faced with breast cancer, a tumour on the brain, a spinal stroke, and everything else in-between and after. It seemed an endless battle for her without much respite. She was told she would never walk again; she learnt to walk again 3 more times. I could write an entire book on all the health challenges she faced. Her medical file was extremely thick, the list of chronic illnesses she had was exceedingly long. One of the greatest gifts she received in her last years was seeing what beautiful humans her grand-children were and the arrival of 4 great grand-children. The bond she had with them all was so special, and they adored her too. She knew that not everyone gets to have this experience and cherished the privilege.

Love and Blessings Always. Fly high sweet Mama. May your overcoming of adversities continue inspiring many that they can be inspirational too.

The Game of Life

The game of life and the meaning and story we create around something. This is a potent energy field. I noticed how healthy it is for us to do this. Have awareness, and in this case, stop yourself before you start. Think another thought, feel another feeling, recall or create a better story, or simply come back to your breath, nothing else just the ebb and flow of your breath.

Interestingly when I was speaking with a client today, he spoke of how he will notice a pattern and do a shift. He would take ownership and change the thought. Another client would do something nice for herself. The outcome is so much better than had either stayed in that pattern and negative space.

The acts can be so simple and the results so much better. Simple to do, yet simple to forget to do, which will you choose? Another reminder is to move. If you're in your head too much, get up and into your body and move it, walk, dance, skip, stretch, exercise, move it, don't lose it.

You can do something as simple as taking a warm shower and putting on a nice outfit. Knowing you are looking good externally can help you course correct internally too. You could simply put on a smile if your ability to move is impaired. The benefits of a smile are covered in the previous chapter: "Experiencing the Shift."

The thoughts you think and the meaning you choose to give to them creates your happiness or sadness; it really is an inside job. I choose this. Through this choosing my dad is with me even more than he could be before. He is one of my angels. He shows up to let me know I'm safe, loved and okay. Every time I see an owl that is him for me. Sometimes he's a bellbird, or a fantail and at other times a song. "Use it or lose it," he would say, and we have so much more available to us, to use.

You can release more of your stories that bring you down. Particularly release those ones that are being hard on yourself, or impatient with yourself. Understand your grieving process, everyone grieves differently and for different lengths of time, there is no right or wrong way. Feelings of guilt, anger, despair and fear are common.

Things You Can Do

• Temporarily scale back your obligations.

• Cry it out (if you want) and don't worry if you don't feel the need to cry.

• Avoid self-medicating such as turning to drugs and alcohol to numb the pain and disconnect from reality.

• Some instead choose short-term medications and remedies to assist in the initial stages to level off emotions and sleep.

• Drinking heavily and giving up on yourself. If you, or someone you know is doing this, seek help from an expert. A detox or counselling programme may be worthwhile also.

• Staying connected to people is a big way to avoid drowning your sorrows alone. You may want to be on your own at some stages. Finding a support group and connecting with others can be a powerful healer too.

• Allow new and more positive memories to overtake the old ones that are causing you pain. Keep developing coping strategies when grief appears. See your thoughts from another loving perspective or replace them with new thoughts that allow you to feel good and enjoy more moments.

• So, when you're ready, get out there and take a chance on yourself to find peace past your pain.

• You never have to get back to "normal," there can now be a new normal. Allow yourself to be stronger than you have ever been in your life, and capable of doing things you were never capable of doing before.

Consoling Another

• Don't let fears about saying or doing the wrong thing stop you from reaching out. Even sharing "I'm not sure what to say, but I want you to know I care."

• Let them know you are there to listen if they want to talk. Simply be there with your support and caring presence.

• Offer to help in practical ways. Running errands, nourishing food, housework, look after their children, or pet's. Make it easy for them e.g. "I'm going to the market, what can I bring you from there?" "I've made a casserole, when can I come by and bring you some?" Take them out for lunch, or a movie. Be there for the long haul with love, compassion, fun and friendship. Be aware their sadness may never completely go away, but the pain can lessen, acceptance and loving life can return.

Connect regularly as a family to find out how everyone is coping:

• Help each other find ways to symbolise, memorialise and

fully express themselves. Go forward with compassion and care, doing the best you know how, until you know better.

Terminal

Diagnosed with a terminal illness: I was so proud of my cousin's attitude and actions as none of us want to be told we only have months to live. We had been texting one another in those last few months and I felt she was here to not only survive, but I could see that she might even shift that survival to carry on and thrive. I was keen to keep supporting her in the background, so she would prove everyone wrong and be another miracle girl.

She is, but not in our living world. To be fair I was gutted. I couldn't change her life path and see her alive. She passed two months prior to my dad. I know the power of love and thought she would prove that to the world by living longer.

Her life path however was different to that and her time in a physical body was to end. This does not mean you give up on the power of love, your thoughts of prayer, of belief, radiating this energy out and beyond. Even of the possibility of a world without death, decline and aging as you currently see and perceive it.

What I am aware of for now is maybe somewhere things shifted, and she became accepting of her journey on this earth plane was to end.

The more awareness you have of yourself and knowing your triggers and how to navigate the paths the better.

The Moral

You have the ultimate choice, and you may not like some of the life lessons you face, but let's just face it with curiosity and humour and see where that takes you. If things are in love and light and that's what you came here to explore more of in an experiential field, let's go have some fun, simply because you can. Pave a new way, create new rules, or maybe we can go beyond rules.

If you are working from that space of unconditional love and no harm to self or others and being very present, miracles are possible. You can use the mantra, "I feel good about this." You then breathe, create, connect, smile, laugh, and accept. You can also forgive, in compassion, in service, beyond your thinking mind and be patient and kind with yourself. If you do all of this, you might even like and appreciate yourself and your part in this world a little more.

"Too much sadness is no good." Dalai Lama

The Dalai Lama shared that statement with us, the people of Christchurch, after our February 22nd, 2011, earthquake. He was on a trip to support those affected by the Christchurch Earthquakes.

The 14th Dalai Lama, Tibetan Buddhist monk Tenzin Gyatso, is the spiritual leader of Tibetan Buddhism and the Tibetan people. He was the first Dalai Lama to become a global figure, largely for his advocacy of Buddhism and of the rights of the people of Tibet. In 1950, he became the head of state of Tibet. In 1959, Chinese troops crushed a full-scale revolt against Chinese occupation. Thousands of Tibetans were killed, and the Dalai Lama and his followers were exiled from Tibet on March 31,1959, fleeing to India.

In 1989, he was awarded the Nobel Peace Prize for his non-violent struggle for the liberation of Tibet. He is also known for his advocacy of peace, human rights, and interfaith understanding. He has consistently advocated policies of non-violence, even in the face of extreme aggression.

Christchurch Earthquakes

I'll take you on a journey of that time. This story is shared to acknowledge what occurred and accept and appreciate what we have. May you release the grief, pain, heartache and live in inspired, loving action as much as you can.

It all started for us on the morning of September 4th, 2010, when we experienced a 7.1 magnitude quake and we rattled about for months (which turned into years afterwards), but we endured, and we adjusted. We felt so grateful that we had withstood it very well and there were no fatalities in that September quake.

We did learn a new word during this time "liquefaction." This was the term used describing the earth bubbling up from underneath. We shovelled big mounds of this smelly silt; we got on with a "new norm" and knew we had a lucky escape.

Then on Boxing Day of 2010, the earth moved right under our city, a 4.9 quake this time. Due to its proximity, it undermined the strength of the buildings in our city centre and at least twenty were damaged as a result. No one had realised a fault line was right beneath us.

Then at lunchtime two months later, under our beautiful city once more, the 6.3 quake struck, and we weren't quite as lucky.

185 fatalities, (including a friend of mine), 1500-2000 injuries, 164 serious had occurred. Structures fell. Our city centre was pretty much destroyed and cordoned off. Our homes were damaged and 600 destroyed. Large areas were red-zoned, (which meant they were now uninhabitable).

While many were feeling anxiety with wounds, mentally and physically, scared, on edge, angry, frustrated, uncertain, and a tirade of other emotions, over in Japan on Friday 11 March a 9.0-9.1 earthquake hit. Not only was there mass destruction and devastation, what followed was a 40.5 metre tsunami.

The events in Japan resulted in 15,894 deaths, 6152 injured and 2563 missing. The very real concerns around the Fukushima nuclear plant were frightening too. This was very sobering and once again we realised how lucky we were in Christchurch.

You do not have to bring mass destruction into your life in any form, whether it be man-made, or through the wrath of Mother Nature.

Let yourself instead be pulled toward that which you do love.

Here is a quote to provide further contemplation. It's from Abraham Hicks. Esther (Abraham and Jerry).

Esther Hicks is an American inspirational speaker, channeler, and author. She has co-written nine books with her husband Jerry Hicks, presented numerous workshops on the law of attraction with Abraham-Hicks Publications and appeared in the original version of the 2006 film The Secret. Known for their profound teachings on the Law of Attraction (LOA), Abraham Hicks explains how our thoughts, feelings, and vibrational frequencies create the reality we experience. This universal principle has inspired millions worldwide to harness their power to manifest joy, success, and abundance. Abraham Hicks says, "a belief is a thought repeated over time." So, pick a new thought and repeat that thought. Now you have a new belief.

On death Abraham Hicks said it's this inevitable new step into a new perspective. It is the continuation of who you are from a more powerful vantage point.

Their Quote:

 "Because we know that life is eternal, and we know that there is no ending to that which you are about, if one of you is killed in an earthquake or crashes your plane, or any number of other very creative ways you have found to make your exit into the Non-Physical, because we know the whole picture, we grieve not a moment for any of you. But from your more short-sighted point of view in physical, a lot of you grieve tremendously."

May we love our lives the best we can. May we have peace and understanding when the physical transforms into the non-physical, and what we call death. May we go beyond all fears and go to that field, the field of human consciousness, cultivating higher states of consciousness, that field of all possibilities.

Wishing you Peace and Love Always.

Even if it may not seem so at times, remember it's all okay. You're in the right place at the right time.

CHAPTER 8: REWIRING AND TUNING IN

"When you think you've reached your peak, you can still reach another." Unknown

Your heart and your higher self, know your business. Have a direct connection here and allow the unfolding from this space and not the external world. You have the power within you.

To rewire your brain and tune in it is helpful to become more aware of what you are doing and saying. Computers are programmed and you are similar. Your experiences in life so far have created programmes, neural pathways that light up, or shut off in your brain.

Stories, judgements and beliefs are wired in your mind and can distort your perceptions. When was the last time you checked in on all those thoughts and messages your mind is sending to you.

When was the last time you asked yourself:

• How true is that now?

• Does this thought serve me?

• What does serve me?

• You can even switch it around and ask, why are things working out so well for me? Why do I feel so good?

Handling Your Hurts

When studies were done on longevity, they looked at a plethora of different diets and cultures. An interesting common theme with the lives of the long-lived people around the world was their ability to handle death of loved ones.

Handling your hurts. How are you doing this?

Call on the simplicity of turning things around.

What if you are facing some challenges?

In this situation it was facing car challenges and a multitude of issues erupted. The person phoned me and shared how everything was going wrong for them. They felt confident it would all be okay but needed help feeling okay about it **now**. I suggested they ask themselves this: "Why is everything working out so well for me with my car **now**?" There may be an initial cringe, if you are not feeling in the space to hear this. You can also try it on and work through the barriers of resistance. The more internal peace and ease they felt about it meant they were able to respond better to what was occurring in their external world.

Notice what you feel and where. Breathe slower and deeper. Give Thanks.

Allow the next right steps and actions to come through and create this "working out well," in your reality too. When you ask the question: "why is everything working out so well," you can reverse engineer the situation. This means once the end goal is established, working backwards to identify the steps needed to reach it. So as if it has already occurred, what were the steps you took to achieve that good result?

With regular practice you can do this shift easier. Creating this shift of thought and bringing good outcomes into the present brings relief and can end the pattern of more bad luck. Things are turning around for her and working out. She is also very grateful, utilising that attribute that allows more goodness in too.

Intention

It can be tough when you see people going through challenges in life. How can you handle such challenges better?

If you are willing, there is a switch that turns the light of positive possibilities on. When you, or you and another know you can do this, miracles can be possible. Wayne Dyer wrote *The Power of Intention* in 2004. In this book he describes intention as "pure, unbounded energy" that is the source of all creation. He also describes intention as a daily practice that can help people turn their dreams into reality.

A few years later, in 2007, investigative reporter, journalist, and author Lynne McTaggart wrote *The Intention Experiment.* She also spoke publicly and appeared on television and radio. Next Lynne created *The Power of Eight* groups and book in 2008. This is where a group of 6 - 12 people, generally like-minded friends who are open to the possibility of healing and intention gather virtually or in person and focus intention healing for others. They choose an intention that benefits all sentient beings and the universe. They sit in silent prayer for about 30 minutes. Lynne said that the groups were so potent that they made her question everything she thought she knew about human nature.

Working with a variety of prestigious scientists and thousands of participants worldwide, she's amassed an extensive body of scientific evidence demonstrating the power of collective intention to make plants grow faster, purify water, lower violence in war-torn areas, heal people of post-traumatic stress disorder and even bring deeply polarised enemies together.

As a researcher, Dr. Joe Dispenza also received his Doctor of Chiropractic degree from Life University, graduating with honours. His postgraduate training covered neurology, neuroscience, brain function and chemistry, cellular biology, memory formation, and aging and longevity. He explores the science behind spontaneous remissions and how people heal themselves of chronic conditions and even terminal diseases. He's more recently begun partnering with other scientists to perform extensive research on the effects of meditation.

Another scientist, this time a globally recognised neuroscientist, medical doctor, international scholar with mastery in both modern science and Vedic wisdom Dr. Tony Nader, has revolutionised the understanding of the mind-body connection and its impact on personal and societal well-being. As a globally recognised expert in the science of consciousness and human development he is also the leader of the Transcendental Meditation organisation.

Tony received his medical degree in internal medicine and his Ph.D. in neuroscience from Harvard and MIT. He worked as a clinical and research fellow at a teaching hospital of Harvard Medical School. He provides the methods, tools, and guidance for connecting with our authentic inner nature and understanding how consciousness is the essence of all existence, including addressing such fundamental questions as:

What is the key to a well-lived, flourishing life in which we can all co-exist in peace?

May you flourish and feel at peace.

Consciousness, that fundamental, limitless and primary force, a vast "unbounded ocean" from which all experiences and realities emerge. That deeper level of pure awareness rather than a product of the brain, or physical matter. Recognise and reconnect with that singularity at the heart of nature.

Make the most of this journey. Find your switch and turn it on daily and look for the light and goodness wherever you can.

Learn your lessons quickly my friend, tune in to the messages and deal with them, life is much easier this way.

Presence

How is your brain currently wired?

Have you unconsciously become addicted to drama, or even your smartphone? Do you turn to your phone anytime there is space, i.e. waiting in line, waiting on someone, or something?

Next time you can choose to resist the temptation to engage with your phone and look up and around you, see your surroundings and start getting present.

Presence is our ability to practice being in stillness, right here right now. The more you practice this the more you step away from your reactionary thoughts and actions. There are addictive qualities in our natures whether it's to our smartphone's or getting angry about someone or something.

The more presence you practice in these moments the more empowered you become. At first the awareness might be after the event, or in the middle, then at the beginning and then you might ask:

• Is this way of dealing with it helpful?

From this you decide:

• Is that behaviour or reaction dysfunctional, or maybe not so intelligent?

You are on your way to another solution and more personal victories and have the freedom of choosing a better way.

What this means is that when bigger challenges do come your way you will be well practiced in presence. You will make more intelligent and less dysfunctional responses.

Using triggers can be a helpful tool in breaking these habits. You could have a phrase each time you are waiting in line, or in traffic.

This phrase is not one of cursing the other person on their poor driving habits. The trigger may even be walking through a door, do this, do that, or let your phone serve you and use it to set reminders to be present. Examples of trigger phrases are:

• If it's to be, the change can start with me.

• I don't have to wait on someone else to change to make me happy.

• I make me happy and radiate this out to the world.

• Every day I improve in each and every way.

Taylor Swift's Song "Shake it off": As she says in her song, "It's like I've got this music in my mind, saying it's gonna be alright..."

Taylor Swift is a singer songwriter and best-selling music artist. Her songs are known for being accessible, distinctive, and heartfelt. She's able to convey feelings, tell stories, and create characters.

It could be good to literally shake off some old habits and ways of thinking that are redundant. Redundant to the you who's here, not just for surviving, or striving, but really thriving.

After this shake off and declaration of what you have now called forth into existence, start giving yourself some gold stars at the time of doing the new habit that you've chosen to do. You could even reflect once a day, and once a week and maybe for the first time really get it that you truly are a loving, caring, powerful creator!

Live in the Vortex

How else can you rewire and tune in? One answer is to live in the vortex:

"Only you can stop your flow of natural wellbeing, look for positive aspects only and eventually only these will be shown to you as you will have incrementally adjusted your vibration and point of attraction. You are a vibration and match to that which you seek, as what comes to you matches you. Focus on the best in others and when characteristics are missing practice seeing them anyway." Esther-Hicks-Abraham

"I've learned that people will forget what you said, people will forget what you did, but people will never forget how you made them feel." Maya Angelou

Maya Angelou, born 4 April 1928, St. Louis, Missouri, United States, suffered violence at home when she was around the age of 7. During a visit with her mother, Maya was raped by her mother's boyfriend. As vengeance for the sexual assault, her uncles killed the boyfriend. Young Maya was so traumatised by the experience that she stopped talking. From her mother she learned to develop courage, and her mother taught this by being courageous herself. Maya realised that one isn't born with courage. One develops it by doing small courageous things - in the way that if one sets to pick up a 100-pound bag of rice, one would be advised to start with a five-pound bag, then 10 pounds, then 20 pounds, and so forth, until one builds up enough muscle to lift the 100-pound bag. It's the same way with courage. You do small courageous things that require some mental and spiritual exertion. Maya worked as a cook, streetcar conductor, waitress, singer, dancer, editor, teacher, civil rights organiser, and actress before becoming one of America's most beloved writers.

What are you to do?

• Reap value from every relationship.

Your Responsibility

• Only your response cuts you off from the good feeling person that you are.

The Focus

• You are not here to shore up others' weaknesses with your strengths, but to pay attention to their strengths which amplifies them.

Having Compassion

• When someone is lashing out in anger, their battle is not with you, but with themselves. It is their personal battle and in time they'll leave you out of it.

Unity

• We share a common thread of source, love and expansion.

Action Steps

• Focus on how you feel about others, not they about you, and discover true freedom.

• Look for positive aspects.

• Keeping the focus on the best you can in others and practice seeing the characteristics that you want to see but are missing.

Achievement

• Practice focusing on the thoughts of the things you desire.

• Appreciation for what is and eagerness for what is coming.

• The relationships you seek are flowing to you. Meet them halfway, relax and enjoy the unfolding.

The Outcome

• Only you can stop the flow of your natural wellbeing.

• There is great love here for you.

Energy Exercises

For more vitality aliveness and clarity of mind try these energy exercises.

• Breathe: Thank you, thank you, thank you. Stand up, stretch up and rub your hands together and shake them off.

• Connecting heaven on earth. Pop your hands on your thighs and then move them to prayer position, palms facing each other. You are just about to do one of the oldest recorded exercises in the world according to Donna Eden. It makes space in the body so healing energy gets where it needs to.

Donna Eden is a pioneer in the field of energy medicine, a holistic healing practice that uses the body's energetic systems to promote health and balance. She's known for her ability to see the body's energies and use them to diagnose and treat physical and psychological issues

• Standing upright, lift one arm with hand flat look up and reach up to the heavens. For your other arm have your hand flat and stretch it down to the earth. With one arm up, the other arm down, stretch and breathe deep.

• Come back to the prayer position with both hands and palms touching. Now reach to the other side, swapping over. Breathe deep each time, in through your nose and release out through your mouth. You can do this a few more times. Or you can simply shift to tapping the acupressure points.

• Start on your cheek bones, great for grounding yourself.

• Then tap on your collar bones, more vitality.

• Your thymus gland strengthening your immune system.

• Your rib cage, at the sides of your body. If you're a woman, it's around your bra line. This is said to metabolise food, thoughts even toxins.

• Now place your right hand on your left shoulder and run it diagonally across the front of your body to your right hip. Then do the opposite side by placing your left hand onto your right shoulder and move it diagonally across your body to your left hip. This is for balancing and integrating the left and right hemispheres of your brain. Nice work.

• Now notice and feel your great energy.

What are you tuning into and gravitating towards?

How can you let this best serve you and your life?

Use the elements to strengthen your spirit and resolve.

- Air - As you breathe in the air or feel the wind on your face.

- Water - As you shower, or watch the rain fall.

- Fire - As you heat up or enjoy the sunshine.

- Earth - As you walk on this ground.

Activate and Integrate

With consistent practice you can activate and integrate these energies, so they become second nature to you.

Air: Intellectual connection, analyse and solve problems. Water: Intuitive and sensitive. Fire: Zest for life, courageous and lively. Earth: Practical grounded and dependable.

"Focus only upon your desires and not upon your fears."

If your fears come up, how would you like it to be, what do you desire? Move into more of this.

- Maybe this is a new skill to learn.

- Maybe there is something others have told you that you're good at.

- Have you been denying this or taking it for granted?

If something comes easy for you, it does not mean that is the case for all humanity. What qualities would your best friend describe as being you? Embrace these and the areas that you do not consider as your natural strengths. You can enhance any area you want to.

Comparing

As humans we tend to compare. If you are doing any comparing it is to compare yourself to the person you were yesterday. If you are comparing yourself to the person down the road, what are the things of great excellence that you aspire to accomplish too? If you are comparing in this way, use it as a yardstick for contrast. How can you close the gap?

Remember to prioritise which areas of your perceived strengths and weaknesses to focus on. What are you focusing on and choosing to spend your time learning and getting good at? These areas are your next strengths.

This may not mean you are going to be, or must be, a gold medallist in the 100-metre sprint. It does mean that you can become quite acceptable at many things you have previously decided that you could not do. Whether it be losing your temper, being intolerant, not being good at public speaking, leadership qualities, or being shy in company. These issues can be remedied with learnable skills for 95% of the population.

Tune in, step back and observe. What do you need to hear right now for your highest good? I was on a walk and saw the word pivot. It's a word I use often, and it reminded me to do that in the moment.

Our Thoughts

There are an estimated 50,000 - 70,000 thoughts we have in a day, and not all of them are our best thoughts. Some research suggests 80% are negative and 98% are the same as the day before. Find relief in that research and realise you're not alone. You can choose to be less critical of yourself and others. I chose to do the pivot into the better ones. Continue to look for the signs and synchronicities, relax and step forward into your best alignment.

One negative belief held, could be: "I'm not loved, and I just know it." The actions and behaviours from this space are more emotional pain and hurt. A belief was planted; it was conceived and took root. It doesn't mean it's real. Remember you don't have to believe everything you think.

A young boy was having a fun time and was excitedly sharing his joy at a family gathering and his father struck him with his hand. The young boy was bewildered, sad and confused. From that day he formed a belief that he was not wanted and felt abandoned.

For you the action could have been that you were shut off in a room, told to shut up, or another situation. What if you made a mess of things back then? You no longer must keep adopting that belief which started there.

You usually start such beliefs when your mind was like a sponge, and you take it all in without the ability to differentiate. These beliefs are commonly happening anywhere between 2 years and 14 years old. Later you may feel embarrassed by your actions, you know better, but can't help it. The hurt, pain, or feeling scared, can be strong. It's as if you are possessed by the 2yr old in you. Don't beat yourself up. The mind can be abusing and scolding, but it does not need to be.

Instead:

 I see you are hurting, and ask how can I comfort you? What do you need to hear right now to stay in alignment? Know your triggers, know what upsets you and send healing to the triggers that exist between you and another.

If you can't handle too much triggering and drama, remove yourself from the situation. Use boundaries until you are past the hurt. Use emotional assessment. Are you calm and happy? You then see yourself back as the adult and in alignment with love rather than sabotaging yourself.

Wayne Dyer would say, "Who am I speaking from?"

Wayne Walter Dyer was an American self-help author and a motivational speaker. Dyer earned a bachelor's degree in history and philosophy, a master's degree in psychology and an Ed.D. (Doctor of Education) in guidance and counselling at Wayne State University in 1970.

Here are some more influential Wayne Dyer quotes to challenge you to be the best version of yourself.

"You don't need to be better than anyone else. You just need to be better than you used to be."

"The greatest gift that you were ever given was the gift of your imagination."

"You are not stuck where you are unless you decide to be."

"The highest form of ignorance is when you reject something you don't know anything about."

"Conflict cannot survive without your participation."

"It's never crowded along the extra mile."

"Everything you are against weakens you. Everything you are for empowers you."

"Judgements prevent us from seeing the good that lies beyond appearances."

The practice of reflecting on any of these quotes daily is a good one. I was also once told, "It means whatever you want it to mean."

At the time of this conversation the inference wasn't one of positivity. It was one of "I'm hinting something negative to you," but I won't spell it out to you. I found it confusing, but the concept is a powerful one of "the meaning we give."

When someone tells you something, it is from their level of consciousness, awareness and understanding. When you drill down with that person, they often cannot come up with the true meaning for you. This may sound like you are going around in circles, but when you cut to the essence, you find the gem.

What is that gem?

The "I do not receive that" is for all the things that bring you harm. Only take what is yours, you can interpret anything anyway you like that best serves you and is doing no harm to you, or others in the process. This is not an avoidance tactic; it's the strategy to use when you have habitually taken on words and responses that have continually caused you harm and saddened your heart.

Reinterpret Your World

Use the negatives to pivot into more positivity of power, growth, loving communication and your own unique brilliance.

Use the positives of others and how they handled themselves to do the same. Emulate the wisest ways of your forbearers.

Seeing Clearly

• If things are fuzzy, what station are you tuned to?

• There could be physical or imagined glasses that you need to clean or change as well.

• Then ask yourself: "What else do I need to accept?"

• If you are unwilling to accept, how can you make your peace with the situation?

Step into feeling better and continue progressing and evolving on your path.

Consider this: when you hurt, the world feels it. There is a saying that "Hurt people, hurt people."

Face your hurt and learn the lessons and gifts that reside in that place for you. Release obligations and play with the joy of what makes your heart sing. At first it may be uncomfortable for others to see you in your power, and they may inadvertently try and hold you back. It may not be so easy for you to recognise yourself in your new power either and outside forces may test you and see if you will drop back. When you truly decide and are ready to simply love and appreciate yourself and them for the parts we are all playing, you can still allow yourself to soar.

They can come with you, the door is open, invite them through.

Are they ready too? If not, let them do their thing and focus on being kind, centred and strong yourself.

You can feel very lucky as there are certain tendencies you come into this world with that can be developed. Mine was a 'sensor', yes, as the word implies, sensitive to things around me. I pick up on things, and that's very exciting, however I did not know how to deal with this.

When I was younger, I chose to bury that side of me, well hide it, as it hurt too much. I was unable to distinguish all these feelings that were coming to me. I thought they belonged to others, but when I tried to share that, they denied those feelings were from them? What I didn't realise was that I was picking up on things before they themselves did, and in some cases they would never.

So, I played in other spaces. The fun one was the 'activator', the social butterfly, and I still like popping into that space often. You can be very surprised when you realise that's not a natural trait of yours. How could that be? You train yourself. You choose what feels good, and you find the areas of "win-win" and coherence between us all.

The moral to this story: Don't let others dictate because they are very clever. You can hold them in high regard, but they do not have all the answers on, or about you. You are so much greater than the tendencies and the genes you've been told you have, or you were born with. You are a limitless being and there is so much more for you to discover.

Relationships Stepping Stones and Tools

As you discover more of yourself and appreciate what is showing up in your life. You appreciate all the relationships as a gift and treat them as the precious insight into love and compassion that is presenting itself. Remember this often and let's see how good you can become at transcending your dislikes and negative judgements of another.

Can you be willing to rewire some more? If you are creating a story let it be something you feel good about today and tomorrow. Great relationships don't happen by chance. You work at them and practice being present. You're not going to be the hurt person who hurts people, whether it be in your words, or actions.

Tune into your Relationships

6 Extra Tips:

1. Give of your best, not your leftovers.

2. To feel satisfied for the long term, be accountable for the part you play in any relationship, good or bad.

3. You are not here to send messages of "who you are is not enough" to others, shame, blame, righteousness, but to seek change in yourself and use open, honest communication using "I" statements of how you feel, rather than "you."

4. Check in regularly with what you appreciate about each other.

5. Repeated practice of all of this and include quality time adding daily fun things too.

6. Remember whatever relationship you are in, first love yourself by taking care of yourself, so you will continue to age with grace and confidence.

Some phrases to help you stay on the right relationship track:

Instead of a reaction like anger, upset or blame, try a gentle way to start a conversation; E.g., I'm curious, puzzled, or confused about what happened with....

Other phrases and responses to recall with meaning are:

• I love you.

• I'm here for you.

• I understand.

- I'm sorry.

- Thank you.

- I really appreciate all that you do.

- It's so nice to see you.

That was quite an accomplishment. Take a big breath in and love the ability to do this.

Clearing

Use another language and some drumming for clearing. Have awareness of your words, body language and tone. Try the possibility of a made-up language coming from your lips, drum a little with your hands on a table and loosen up your body of any tension held. Imagine that you're clearing anything that isn't here for your highest good and best, most fun loving, kind, powerful expression. The drumming can be clapping or tapping, get a beat and some movement happening. You can also add an audio segment, creating more fun, playfulness and you might love the rhythm too.

You look for your next peak, what could be yours? Rewire and tune in.

Remember it's all okay. You're in the right place at the right time.

CHAPTER 9: KICKING FEAR AND WORRY TO THE CURB

"Be the reason someone believes in the goodness of people."
Unknown

Do you find that you tend to get hard on yourself when you are not feeling good 100% of the time, or 90%, or even 80%? Irritation, blame and worry can occur if you are not in the right mindset, or have the right attitude.

When and why do you quit something?

The most common reason for someone to quit a job is because there is one person that they really don't like. All the other aspects of the job may be great, but they quit because of one. The tendency is to avoid challenging emotions of life. What if you instead decided for at least 55% of the day, "I choose to feel better, glad, eager, fulfilled, satisfied, complimentary, and release the ornery, irritation, worry, or blaming for today."

Be mindful of the choices you are making today. Are they from a place of love, or fear? Are you fearful of repercussions if you don't act aggressively, or from habit? If this is the case, you can reframe and re-choose.

Connection

We are made from nature, when we are in and with nature greater ease and alignment is available as we are with the sun, the moon, the stars, and the seasons. Be in sync with these. You are not meant to be in full bloom throughout the year, you want to bloom and sow good seeds to bloom and blossom again. So, if you are struggling with anything right now, let go of the struggle and just be with what it is you are experiencing.

Yes, it can feel difficult and unpleasant, take a walk outside and recalibrate. Release the tension and set the intention of what you're choosing to set up and experience next. You can also call upon nature, your angels, or whatever it is that is a source of love and strength for you.

Ask for strength, call upon your loved ones and ask for help, ask the universe for answers, yes, but don't push to get out too quickly, life is happening for you.

There are lessons and messages for you. What could they be? The man that felt sorry for the butterfly that was caught in its cocoon, cut it open to help, and the butterfly fell out and died, because it wasn't finished transforming.

One of your greatest gifts is to be patient, patient with yourself as you are learning your life's lessons, and transforming that learning into more love, joy and appreciation of all that is.

As you listen to the callings of your body, doing your next steps, you may find yourself stepping into being divinely guided, tapping into your inner wisdom and its guidance more powerfully. Noticing you're like the seasons. Honouring it all. The seeding, the watering, the sprouting and growing, the flowering, fruiting and a new crop of seeds.

Tune in to the unique phases moving from pushing and trauma responses of fight, flight, freeze, into nurturing, nourishing and kindness - established in the self and refining your intellect. Moving from silence to dynamism. Keeping your rest and digest separate. Working in harmony with the seasons and enacting healthy living rituals.

Healthy Living Rituals

What are some of these healthy living rituals?

• Starting your day with water, fresh unadulterated pure water.

•Meditating or listening to music that inspires you for 5

minutes.

• Eating just enough breakfast to get you to lunch.

• Keep flowing.

• A dynamic meal at lunch. (Our digestive fire is linked to the sun).

• A controlled breathing practice - such as a 3-part breath, or alternate nostril breathing.

• An afternoon reset, even if it's just for 5 minutes. Get your attitude readjusted, your mind and body enlivened and yourself re-inspired.

• Go into your next hour with passion and purpose. Do this reset and intention action more often if you find you're having energy drops.

Adequate hydration is a simple start for the day, wake up, stretch up and go drink a large glass of water. How many people are doing this? Are you making things more complicated than they need to be?

Repetitive Cycles and Breaking the Cycle

I read a short article about a Palestinian boy who was a suicide bomber. He was captured and the bomb not detonated, they had killed his friend, and he wanted to kill them and himself because of it.

His automatic reaction was disrupted, and the cycle was broken, and nobody else died.

You are the change you seek. You can stop these repetitive cycles of sadness, anger and war by changing your reaction to these people and yourself. More killing results in more killing. This means more death and despair for even more people. This pause, this change of action, stops the normal chain of events, throws a spanner in the works and breaks the normal escalating pattern.

We all act out if we feel we haven't been seen, heard, appreciated and loved somewhere in our lives.

That other person may not realise the effect your little acts of kindness can have, never underestimate how you can be unstoppable in positive life enhancing loving ways.

What little act of kindness, what beautiful ripple in the ocean can you start now and strengthen? What one nice thing can you do each day?

What is the nice thing you have done today to show your love for yourself, mankind and the planet?

Here's one simple act and answer to that:

• "I picked up some rubbish from the pathway."

What else can, could, and are you choosing to do? It doesn't matter how small the act, it is all worthwhile and does make a difference.

Even if your enthusiasm fades a little during the day, take a moment release the tension and set another intention and show an action toward that. What if you make this little positive shift each day and keep making it? Bring your "A" game to all areas of your life.

Changing a Normal Reaction

To change a reaction into a wiser response. Have a system for when you notice yourself dropping into old habits that no longer serve you. Know that it can start with the little things and can snowball from there. You can go straight for the big things, as long as you keep carrying on and practice these out of the box responses. One tool a client had was to ping a rubber band on their wrist to remind themselves they were doing that "thing" again, and from this, they changed the pattern.

Do practise the skills and trust in your ability to change your sails if need be. Use your courage to do the best action, rather than staying stuck in a belief system of: "This is how it must be done."

We are all learning and evolving. This means it's okay to "not feel okay and have doubt and fear shake your foundations for a little while," just choose not to stay in that place too long. Seek clarity, learn from this and make your next bold move.

"If in doubt write it out." Writing and journaling are great ways to keep it real, or making the real have a positive spin, looking for the good in it, or the possibility of good from it.

• How can I add value here?

•How can I show up, so I get to experience fulfilling interactions?

• What could go wrong and how could I deal with it?

No matter what, I'm going to be okay. This or something even better is unfolding and I am grateful for it.

Let Beauty In

Facing your difficulty and pain and let beauty in while you are suffering. The pain lives in us rather than us in the pain. Fears of pain and the unknown enlarge the sense of things when in pain.

Keep learning and working with it, endless practice, just like you never want to be done with breathing.

The more you don't look and ignore something the bigger it gets, instead face everything and rise. In time you grow accustomed, and you see into it. If you are in pain or fear, look directly at it until your heart and mind can see what is there. When in fear, or pain respect yourself by looking again at what you are afraid of and fears you. Respect looks again. It's inside you; you don't need to look away. Personal work on yourself is healing and is about looking and moving through it. You've got this!

Facing What Is

Mark Nepo had cancer in his 30's. He believes it does not have to be catastrophic. It can be beauty, wonder, surprise and passion. It can be as beautiful, or as difficult as you make it, and spiritual journeys can begin. The ages of 33-36 were difficult for him with bouts of cancer and he nearly died. This helped him formulate his philosophy of experiencing life fully, while staying in a relationship with an unknowable future.

Though this was a challenging reality to face, you do not have to face despair to have your breakthroughs. Embrace whatever is and move through it, even though instinct is to run away. Choose to lean back in. See things as they are, and more choices can arise.

Very simple things can be applied, using the philosophy of:

• "Simple disciplines rather than simple errors in judgement."

Keep moving towards that which you wish to see. Practice the good habits of someone who has achieved that wish already and close the gap.

Safety and Fear

Reminders are here for you to receive the message beyond the words. There is a ring of safety around you.

We were walking in the hills, and a honeybee stung my husband on the foot, through his sock. The bee was exhausted from the ordeal and my husband was in pain. The automatic response could have been squash and kill the bee, but we paused and thought again. The bee was only reacting to its legitimate danger, being squashed up against a shoe. I removed the bee from the sock and left it curled up recovering.

Considerations

• Where is your line of legitimate safety and where is your line of extended fear?

• Who are you closing out?

• What are you not doing, or saying because your ring of fear is extended?

• What step might you take to bring them closer together to make things more congruent?

Respect yourself and look again. See what is hurting you and move through it.

You are creating your realities. You become untouchable and you become lonely, if you are extending the ring of fear too far.

Finding the Point

In Martial Arts such as Aikido, if you look at the energy of fear, the energy of the aggressor is to sweep it past you. The master teaches the apprentices to fear the cloud of alarm e.g. a knife, the toe, they equal fear. You can outweigh the cloud of the alarm in a few seconds in your inner life, so look at that person and outweigh the cloud of alarm. Sweep it by you. In Aikido there is only one point threatening you and that is the end of the knife, all the other points are safe. One spot, what a relief.

An antagonist could fear insecurity e.g. no job, losing a love, fear of facing surgery, I don't really love myself. Respect yourself and look at the "point" of the threat and as you do it is no longer overwhelming, and a big thing out there separate to you. You have real choices and can choose what steps you take next. Maybe you can handle this, get through this, and even have the elegance to dance through life. What would it take?

Inflate and Deflate

Just because you know this doesn't mean you will do this. You may get dropped into the depths of life and feel overwhelmed at first. There is a rhythm of inflation, making things appear worse, but let inflation subside and see it as it is there. The cloud of alarm may overcome you again. You do have decisions to make, when it inflates, outweigh it, right size it (deflate it) and now meet it. Reframe. Accepting your wholeness rather than seeking perfection.

Living Wholeheartedly

Each breath can set us free. If you are confused or worrying, no amount of thinking can get you out. Dropping it, hold nothing back and lean into what is before you. You will then see clearly again.

• How sensitive are you after you've been offended?

• How safe you can feel after you've been afraid?

• How certain you can become after doubt?

It can be a messy magnificent journey being human. The light within your interaction with the world reveals itself. You now have clear eyes and a different decision to the problem that was before you.

Feelings are your greatest resource, practice and lean in. In that fight or flight waves swell and dip again and again, so do you. It is important not to be self-critical when pulling back, overcome with fear; it's the nature of being human. What happens next, such as kindness to yourself and others matters.

Even with this knowledge and awareness, you can be concerned that there are times you feel dullness and sadness. At such times it's good to release all guilt, as you may harbour this readily.

A Louise Hay phrase, "I love and approve of myself", is handy to repeat.

Sometimes you expect to be feeling even better and can be surprised that there are times you still feel vulnerable with sadness and insecurities. You also know this too will pass and if you like, you can let it happen more purposefully.

Part of your work is to notice your strength through how you are being. This "being" is to be more loving and gentler, more open and allowing with yourself. You can integrate your unique feminine and masculine parts of yourself. Often, as a form of protection, you may have become dominant in one over the other.

As you do this and become more integrated in your full power, you lighten up and find yourself communicating with kind, positive, loving transfers; what a pleasant relief.

What has opened in you is more important than what opened you e.g. if you were betrayed or treated unjustly. How can you rise to be more than this?

You are powerful, grateful, and in loving awareness. Here you find yourself thankful for all your life experiences.

Growth from Negative Experiences

I have heard many stories where people could easily not have trusted and loved again, but instead they showed us the way and live beyond the persecution and traumatic events they survived. You think it would be too hard for them to believe that "life loves us," but they do. Now they see it in their reality and experiences. Their life is one of thriving not merely surviving. The opportunity to see that reflected to them has finally arrived. They had the vision for greatness. They let it in and didn't give up.

Auschwitz

I listened to a lady speak of the horrors she faced in Auschwitz. She spoke of the two camps of people afterwards. One lot were survivors and thrivers and the other survivors still trying to survive, they were caged in their own minds. The difference she noticed was their attitude, living forward and not retreating.

Man's Search for Meaning is a 1946 book by Viktor Frankl.

Viktor Frankl (1905-1997) is known for founding logotherapy, a school of psychotherapy that focuses on finding meaning in life. He was also a Holocaust survivor. Frankl's theory is that people are motivated to find meaning in life, and that psychotherapy should help people find that meaning. He was a professor of neurology and psychiatry at the University of Vienna Medical School.

His book chronicled his experiences as an Auschwitz concentration camp inmate. He explores the search for meaning, the power of love, and finding humour and courage in difficult times. This led him to discover the importance of finding meaning in all forms of existence, even the most brutal ones, and thus, a reason to continue living. He chose to find purpose in life that he could feel positively about, and then actively imagining that outcome.

Hiroshima

In Japan I listened to a man speak of his experiences in Hiroshima, he was just a Little Boy at the time. We listened to the atrocities that occurred and the challenges he faced. He along with many others, faced extreme adversity, not only were they treated as outcasts, but they had many ongoing health conditions from that day. That day was August 6, 1945, when the United States dropped the atomic bomb "Little Boy" on Hiroshima. It was the first city to be hit by an atomic bomb. The bombing destroyed more than 10 square kilometres of the city. The heat from the bomb created fires that lasted for days. The immediate death toll was between 60,000 and 80,000 people. However, many more died from radiation sickness in the years following the bombing. That little human boy was a survivor and thriver.

Learn from the mistakes of the past and do not bring them through to your future and blind you from the goodness that can be.

Mahatma Gandhi .

When in India I visited the place where Mahatma Gandhi was assassinated. It was a very moving experience, and I was reminded of many of his profound messages including:

"An eye for an eye makes everyone blind."

Mohandas Karamchand Gandhi (1869-1948) was an Indian lawyer, politician, social activist, and writer who employed nonviolent resistance to lead the successful campaign for India's independence from British rule. He inspired movements for civil rights and freedom across the world. This, from being a very shy young child running home as soon as school ended to avoid talking to anyone. In 2007, the United Nations declared Gandhi's birthday, October 2nd, as the International Day of Non-violence.

You can have an even brighter future. Never give up on this. You may now have that knowingness that life loves you and you are here to thrive, you can also move forward with the realisation that: "Life is happening for you" and not to you.

You can be okay with all the feelings you face; you can also be realistic, and as Wayne Dyer would say:

"Be realistic and expect miracles."

Some feelings and experiences may be uncomfortable, but you can "move through them," rather than up against them.

Sometimes in life, you are sowing seeds and watering them, only to see all the weeds come up. What if there is a better way, a shift of focus?

Dealing with Weeds

The saying, "a weed is but an unloved flower" means that a plant considered a weed is essentially just a flower that is not desired in a particular location. This is often because it is growing where it is not wanted by humans, making it "unloved" despite potentially having aesthetic qualities like any other flower.

Moeraki Boulders in New Zealand are geological marvels, they're huge spherical boulders scattered on the beach. There is a short walk through regenerating native bush down to them at the beach. Gorse here in New Zealand is a weed that takes over, it's persistent and there used to be a lot of it. Originally brought in for use as hedges, the gorse loved the climate and spread uncontrollably. What they can successfully do in Moeraki is plant native vegetation in a way that the gorse does not get to see the light. This reduces growth, eventually causing the root system to die.

As you devotedly sow seeds, what you reap could be disappointing, there may be too many weeds appearing instead. "As you sow, so shall you reap" is a proverb that means your present actions will shape your future. It's often used to describe how your behaviour will affect how others treat you. If you sow kindness, you will reap kindness. If you sow a lie, you will reap a quarrel or slander.

As you breathe inwardly there is a sacred space, protected and honourable. You are giving attention and getting attention a negotiation is taking place. Your life is giving to you and it is coming from what you are giving attention to. It's a blessing to feel congruent and at peace inwardly.

In this peace you are also aware that out in the world there is friction and various weather conditions, but with this inner peace you can handle it with grace and calm. You are like the ocean rarely still. Instead of stillness, you and the ocean can be churned up, that is, until you go deeper where stillness resides.

Allow your fears to subside and let more of your goodness through. Kick your worry to the curb and smile again.

Remember it's all okay. You're in the right place at the right time.

CHAPTER 10: LIFE LESSONS: BUSINESS, SPORT, AND HEART

"Don't lose hope. When the sun goes down, the stars come out."
Unknown

You can be a heart centred leader in business and sport. Before the approach was one of living more in the mind. Mistakenly we believed this was serving our heart, but what if it is the other way around? Operate from the inside out not outside in.

Keep a cool mind and a warm heart.

Eleanor Roosevelt said: "To handle yourself, use your head; to handle others, use your heart." As wife of President Franklin D. Roosevelt, Eleanor (1884-1962), played a key role in leading the nation through two national crises, the Great Depression and World War II. Through her activism and post-war diplomacy, she was also instrumental in the development of civil and human rights for all people.

A heart-centred leader benefits from increased employee engagement, loyalty, and productivity due to their focus on empathy, compassion, and genuine care for their team members, fostering a positive work environment that promotes creativity, innovation, and overall well-being within the organisation. This type of leadership can also lead to a stronger company culture and reputation, attracting and retaining top talent. Leaders who lead with heart can actively shape a company culture that values integrity, kindness, and respect.

When leaders are primarily leading "from the mind," they rely heavily on logic, data, and analytical thinking without considering emotions or interpersonal dynamics. Potential problems include lack of empathy, poor communication, difficulty adapting to change, low team morale, resistance to new ideas, and an inability to inspire or motivate others. Essentially, they are creating a cold, detached leadership style that may struggle to connect with their team on a deeper level.

Heart-Centred Leadership

Important Aspects:

1. Active listening: Truly listening to employees' concerns and perspectives.
2. Open communication: Sharing information transparently and honestly with the team.
3. Positive reinforcement: Recognizing and celebrating individual achievements.
4. Emotional intelligence: Understanding and managing one's own emotions, as well as the emotions of others.
5. Authenticity: Leading with genuine values and beliefs.

Mind-First Leadership

6 Key Issues - How to Mitigate These:

1. Develop emotional intelligence: Actively work on understanding and managing emotions, both in themselves and others.
2. Practice active listening: Pay attention to non-verbal cues and actively seek out different perspectives.
3. Foster open communication: Encourage open dialogue and create a safe space for team members to share their thoughts and concerns.
4. Balance logic with intuition: Consider both data-driven analysis and gut feeling when making decisions.
5. Delegate effectively: Trust team members with autonomy and responsibility to make decisions.
6. Show appreciation and recognition: Acknowledge individual contributions and celebrate successes to boost morale.

The Approach to Life of Leading from the Heart

The heart generates the largest electromagnetic field in the body. In the Electricity of touch experiment performed by Heartmath they measured an exchange of energy between people, their findings were: "When people touch, or are in proximity, a transference of the electromagnetic energy produced by the heart occurs." The Heartmath institute has researched and developed reliable, scientifically based tools, to help people bridge the connection between their heart and minds and deepen connections with the hearts of others.

People, countries and cultures have different belief systems. The ways that they feel are appropriate in communicating and doing business may not gel well for you. How do you understand that they too are doing their best in their unique way? The belief and phrase that "we are all one" embodies a fundamental concept which can be found in various religious, spiritual, and philosophical traditions, including Hinduism, Buddhism, Quantum Physics and Yoga. It signifies that everything in the universe is interconnected and fundamentally part of a single, unified consciousness; this idea is often referred to as "oneness."

Oneness: We Are All One, But Not the Same - Yoga Journal.

When you look underneath the differences in external appearance, the same essence is under everything. From this awareness of the oneness of us all, what is your heart centred approach?

New Zealanders

New Zealanders were known for having a can-do approach. The number 8 wire mentality was a term popularised in the 1980's. It was also known as kiwi ingenuity. Then it referred more to the men, particularly country folk and farmers, (those who made their living from the land and whose remoteness meant they had to rely on themselves a bit more than most).

This is how I grew up. My dad was very resourceful and could turn his hand to most jobs, because he had to. To survive you had to skill up, there was no mechanic down the road to go to, you were it. You had to give it a go, learn how it was done, and do your best, it was a necessity. Generally New Zealanders were known as practical, lateral thinking, problem solving types, capable of inventing, or fixing anything with whatever junk they had lying around in the garden shed. The number 8 wire is a gauge of steel wire used for fencing paddocks.

New Zealanders can come across quite laid back in their attitudes and approach. This is changing as we become more of a multicultural society. It was a very endearing trait and did not mean we were not performing at high levels. It can mean that a lot of today's marketing and the focus on more money is not the approach to inspire your average New Zealander.

Lifestyle, freedom and choice inspires many worldwide. This is about more than having more money: it's how we treat one another in the process, our ethics and honesty.

Failure is Not Failure

Remember supposed crazy people giving it a go, this attitude got man on the moon. Be new and different. Be prepared to give it a go, focus on what you do have and can do, rather than a wall of no. Trying, trying and trying again, perfecting your art.

"I have not failed. I've just found 10,000 ways that won't work." Thomas Edison

Thomas Edison (1847-1931) was a prolific inventor and businessman who held a record 1,093 patents. He's known for inventing the incandescent light bulb, the phonograph, and alkaline batteries. He was also a leader in the development of motion pictures.

Sir Peter Jackson, New Zealand filmmaker, is best known as the director, writer and producer of the Lord of the Rings trilogy, and the Hobbit. He is (2017) the second-highest grossing director at the worldwide box office ($6.52 billion).

In an interview I heard about the number of times the studio executives in LA would start panicking and get on the phone to Peter's agents becoming a running theme. When they were asking Peter how the cut was going on the film, he would be replying "yeah nah it's pretty good, it's coming together and looking pretty good." To them he was sounding less than enthused that this is going to work.

They were concerned as to how committed he was of delivering this for them. He was sounding too laid back. His agent would be contacted to ask Peter: "What's wrong? Is there a problem with the production?" He would answer, "No, why?

You may not necessarily be the loudest, or first one to put your hand up to say: "We've got this," but do not misinterpret this. You too can have a willingness to impress and give of your best. You too may have a tendency of letting your actions speak louder than your words, and not the other way around.

High achievers in New Zealand often have a reputation of understating their achievements. You don't have to look far to see examples of this. The late Sir Edmund Hillary, conqueror of Everest and the All Blacks (ABs) constantly demonstrate such an attribute. The All Blacks are our NZ rugby union team, who are statistically the best side to have ever played the game.

As the most successful international men's rugby side of all time, they have a winning percentage of 76.77% over 637 Tests played between 1903 and 2023.

So many captains and players (such as former AB captain Richie McCaw) show these same traits.

Mindset

• Belief. You believe this is possible

- Determined

- Wanting to excel

- Getting on with it

- Getting the job done

- Giving of your best where you are

- This was about something bigger than you and you knew it.

The accolades they received as a result were not their driving force. They were humble in their acceptance, not wanting the spotlight of attention, but knowing the importance of celebrating these victories too.

Take courage and let your actions match your words and your goodness.

Meeting World Emotions

You may be a runner and there is an uneven surface, and you trip, luckily only scraping your knee. This could mean ouch and perhaps your reaction is an instant swear word leaving your lips. That's where you get up and lean in.

Often a plaster is all that is needed to heal the wound. But what if you take it further and are annoyed at yourself for tripping in the first place or for swearing afterwards. What if you were in a race and missed out on a medal. What if you start getting very critical of yourself, and are dwelling in the darkness and the situation keeps getting worse, then what?

There is a quote by Maharishi Mahesh Yogi: "Water the root to enjoy the fruit."

This is about nourishing the source, an analogy that compares the root of a tree to a person's inner consciousness. A strong foundation is needed for a sturdy structure. Perhaps with this you will fall less, or if you do, you can respond better.

Responding in a more thoughtful considered action, taking a moment to process, rather than reacting and acting in an immediate, instinctive, and potentially emotional way to a situation that is impulsively based on an initial feeling or stimulus.

Having anxiety about the worst-case scenario is also called catastrophising. This is our brain's way of believing we're keeping ourselves safe and preventing uncertainties from derailing us. However, the irony of catastrophising is that it's what makes our anxiety worse. Instead, be more specific, get to the point and water that root. A healthy root system is needed for a tree to flourish. Inner silence is the basis for successful activity. Transcending mental activity can lead to clarity, peace, and broadened awareness. Here you are rising above and going beyond, turning on your inner light of awareness, this can reduce the struggle. Lean in, you are so much more.

It's how you react next, face it and lean in, as the space that is held for you is not one of pain and suffering, anguish and doubt, guilt or fear. You no longer dwell in these spaces for as long as you did in the past. Instead, you find yourself moving through this better than before. You practice marinating in this wisdom of possibility, receiving the lessons as gifts and seeing what else can now be.

Binge listen and binge heal if you choose. Engage in amazing content, or with people who you feel great to be around, or with yourself, excited and feeling good. As you allow yourself to move into and know your beautiful power, your wisdom and the light you are, you allow the mastery and become more masterful at being in joy.

Success Pyramid

 John Wooden created a powerful basketball dynasty and used what he called the "Success Pyramid" to achieve that. Earlier we talked of "Success Settings" and now we are going to look at the pieces that make up John's "Success Pyramid."

The Success Pyramid:

• Industriousness.

• Friendship, loyalty.

• Co-operation and enthusiasm.

• Self-control, alertness, initiative, and intentness.

• Condition, skill and team spirit.

• Poise and confidence.

• Competitive greatness.

Muhammad Ali, three-time world heavyweight boxing champion would say: "It isn't the mountain ahead to climb that wears you out, it's the pebble in your shoe."

It's all about you, yourself, if you are ready, everything else will fall into place; your race, your background, it doesn't matter.

You may already have a day planned. Your thinking mind knows what you have in store, but the day may take you off on another path.

Disruption

 To see how willing, flexible and able you are to handle this well: Have you faced what might trip you up? Have you trained your mind and body how to overcome such obstacles?

The Crusaders, a Super Rugby Franchise in Canterbury New Zealand, had a game plan. They had practised and were prepared for the team they were to meet. Scott Robertson, their head coach spoke to the media afterwards and said, "We didn't do anything that we hadn't planned or trained for." They also managed to win and win well.

Why? There are many answers for this and many great rugby pundits sharing their insights. Some key findings were that their team culture was really established, great strength, fitness, strategy and leadership. There was also depth in their group. They were getting the basics of the game right, playing to their capabilities, with great defence and attack. They had enough wisdom and clarity to be flexible with their original game plan and adjust well. They also knew the game plan that was needed to play to the conditions.

They allowed their greatness to come from them in the moments, because they had trained for this, they had the skills, knowledge, power and belief. They knew they had the ability to bring this forth. That knowing was deep down in them and they let it shine in their game. They knew they had whatever it took within them to succeed. In the lead up and in that game that faith never wavered long enough to let defeat win.

The outcome for the Crusaders that 2017 season: they were crowned the Super Rugby champions with their final victory over the Lions in Johannesburg, South Africa.

Your Frequency

You have the ability; your frequency can rise. Activate your own sense of purpose, we each carry the light. In the darker lower frequencies, every act of kindness and gratitude shifts it higher and lighter too.

Most know that radio frequencies are used to transmit information through radio waves, knowing this as we tune to different stations to hear the station we like. Higher frequencies mean shorter wavelengths and potentially higher quality transmission. The vibrational energetic state or level of a person has higher frequencies which are often associated with positive emotions and higher consciousness.

According to David Hawkins higher frequencies correspond to positive states like love and peace, while lower frequencies represent negative states like fear and anger. This was a map of consciousness developed by David R. Hawkins, M.D., Ph.D. (1927 - 2012). He was director of The Institute for Spiritual Research,

Inc. He was also a renowned psychiatrist, physician, researcher, spiritual teacher and lecturer.

We may ask, which station are you tuned to? I hear love and above is a pretty good one. Where you feel on the scale may fluctuate and how you perform may too. You may be a high performing sports person, or not, running your own successful business, or not, in a career or job you love, or not, a mum, a dad, a daughter, a son, a friend, no matter how you may label yourself, or not, how good you are feeling, or not, that you're here means you are important, valued and there is more good to come.

Making a Difference

A lovely gentleman wanted to acknowledge a lady, to let her know how he appreciated her. It was a heartfelt gesture from him. Many of us have good thoughts we want to share with others in our mind, but don't.

He went the extra mile "literally" and the next day let her know how he appreciated that interaction. She had taken the time to call out and speak to him. She replied, "I was just being kind," but her face told a different story; it lit up and she was smiling, and very pleased to receive the compliment. He was reminding her that the little acts of kindness she was doing, do make a difference. It made her day, and in so doing he too felt even better for making the effort to acknowledge her. It solidified in him, the importance of how these little things can have a beautiful impact.

Too often we underestimate our power to create positive change, simple actions creating a positive ripple effect. It may be this practicing kindness towards another, being mindful of where we are spending our shopping dollar and what businesses we are supporting, volunteering our time, conserving energy, reducing, recycling and reusing, donating to charity, being mindful of water usage, the products we are using, the words we are saying, listening actively to others, and speaking up or showing up in our own best ways for causes we believe in. Here making this world and even better place together.

Life's a mystery, there's so much we don't know. Keep leaning in and listening to your highest calling. If you are feeling in unfamiliar territory, the quote from Napoleon Hill can provide some solace and relief: "Every failure brings with it the seed of an equivalent success."

What's the best thing for you, us, to do right now, for the greatest good?

You have shifted, roll up your sleeves, with a sense of urgency, it's time. You're not panicked or alarmed; it's simply time to get out of your own way. A reminder along the path was to teach people how to treat you, rewrite the rules and create new higher standards.

• "You can only be treated the way you let people treat you."

This statement came up in an interview Oprah Winfrey had with Reese Witherspoon.

Reese Witherspoon is an Academy Award winning actress and producer. She co-founded the media company Hello Sunshine in 2016 with Seth Rodsky. Reese started the company because she was frustrated with the lack of opportunities for women in Hollywood.

Being in Alignment

When your beliefs are in alignment with your decisions, your behaviours also match. How you act speaks louder than the words you say, of how you think you act.

To check in on this here are some things to consider:

• What is it you intend to do and what do you do?

Many of us are unconsciously sabotaging ourselves. This can be because of an underlying belief that you can't do it, or feel that it is not possible, or maybe you simply don't want it enough. Check in with yourself of what you believe is possible versus, what you want to achieve?

Shining the light of awareness here has you mending and building bridges.

Are you now building the bridge and picturing yourself during and just after you've realised your dream too? Are you feeling the uncertainty and doubt, acknowledging those feelings and seeing ways how you can be in the energy of solutions overcoming the challenges and moving into joy, bliss, happiness and even more gratitude? It can be a bumpy ride at times, but you can soften your response and let go of resistance.

Having your 'North Star' in life, a guiding principle, a personal vision, or a core value that acts as a constant reference point, providing direction and purpose in your life. It's much like the actual North Star in the sky helping navigators find their way.

Have your long-term goal or aspiration that keeps you focused even when faced with challenges or uncertainty.

This might give you a jolt, as you face your deep-down beliefs. These may not be what you thought you thought, but your actions and activations. Society, culture, the beliefs held to be true, are getting a good look at. There can be interesting shifts in your goals, work, career and changes of focus and priorities. All that is occurring in our world can feel very unsettling, but many of you reading and hearing this now are in this knowing that there is something more and better to tune into. This is regardless of what may be showing up externally trying to convince us otherwise. You are coming back here to be reminded and establishing yourself further into your own unique brilliance, each of us making a difference to the collective coherence. Allowing these words to activate more of the amazing awesome light of you and us.

Here in Harmony

What you were doing in the world has shifted. You are now aware of the lower aspect, aware of the frustration and irritable times that were once all too frequent.

Your learning and growth mindset means you've already done your best, you acknowledge and understand that you're still learning and will and can do better this week, compared to last week. Use these skills you have acquired and are acquiring throughout your lifetimes.

A young man grew up with three brothers, he was older but seemed weaker. He had a different disposition to the others. They thought they were being kind to him by not including him in physical activities. Later in life he started to experience issues with swelling in his body. He was holding onto these fears from the past, missing out and being left out.

Yes, there may have been other areas he could improve with his lifestyle, food, exercise and mind habits, but it was also time for him to release those hurts of the past. Everyone is doing the best they know how from their level of consciousness, forgive them and forgive yourself for holding onto those fears for so long.

It's not the attention you crave and need; it's simply the love. Come from your heart space. You must give this love to yourself first, which means you can then radiate out even more love and kindness to others.

Yes, you may be more experienced in an area, but we are all equal regardless of how much darkness or light we carry – we all require unconditional love. We can be here in harmony.

Exploring New Ground

In the late 1990s Larry Page and Sergey Brin realised that the sprawling, chaotic mass of material that was cascading onto the World Wide Web could be tamed by ranking search results according to their popularity.

They pulled together $1m from family, friends and other investors. Their company, now known by billions as Google (parent company Alphabet), was launched on 7 September 1998.

They haven't looked back, making millions from online advertising and embracing some of the most challenging new ideas in the world of technology.

Alongside nurturing the growth of the search engine, they were always eager to explore new ground.

Google has a famous "20% time," which allows employees to take one day a week, for some blue sky thinking, on original projects. This has produced some great new innovations. Yet not everything has worked, and they, like the rest of us, keep learning and moving forward.

Whether it is in business, sport, living from your heart, or all of the above, you are one of the stars and can explore more too.

Remember it's all okay. You're in the right place at the right time.

CHAPTER 11: DOING YOUR BEST AND HANDLING OVERWHELM

"Keep away from people who try to belittle your ambitions. Really great people make you feel that you too, can become great." Mark Twain

Mark Twain (1835 - 1910) is the pen name of Samuel Clemens. He was an American humourist, journalist, lecturer and novelist. Best known for books such as *The Adventures of Tom Sawyer* (1876) and *Adventures of Huckleberry Finn* (1885). Clemens operated riverboats, and mark twain is a nautical term for water found to be two fathoms (12 feet [3.7 metres]) deep: mark (a measure) twain (number two).

Becoming Great

This is a great "bust out your journal" chapter. Write down more great tips to use and remember to take advantage of them, using what serves you best.

What if you're feeling overwhelmed and don't know where to start or have many projects and feel too busy. Pick one area or one thing, just start there, doing your best. We can't undo yesterday all you've got is today. Put 100% effort into what you are doing. Do the best you can, that's all.

Tomorrow hasn't arrived yet, you do have today, make each day your masterpiece, have a big goal that matters and excites you. If you're not sure what it is yet, follow some of your passions, or things you enjoy doing. See the picture, feel the joy, the bliss, the excitement, the phenomenal gratitude and delight. Live into the possibility and start seeing the little signs that are showing up. These may initially seem as if they're for others, when they are signs of reminders of what you are asking for. It's on its way to you. This can turn out far better than you can imagine. Keep open to your miracles and positive possibilities coming from this.

The full delivery may not arrive today or tomorrow. Keep moving forward, seek, see and thank the small signs that are showing up, related to your desire. Trust your guidance, your joy meter in life, become good at using it. Yes, you may still have days, or situations that challenge you a little or a lot, I still get them too.

This surprised me at first, as if I wasn't doing "it" right (whatever that "it" was meant to be). We are bouncing forward quicker and better than ever before, learning and growing more. Your light may be flickering off and on, eventually staying on longer. It's like a strong muscle you're working on. Make a difference, be the best you. You are developing as a human being every day.

Doing your best is a choice. You may not feel your best, just take command of your attitude that day and do your best. Live by the gift of life, doing the best you can, influencing people you can.

Success experts have greater integrity, loyalty and are not chasing the next things. They are not falling into the trap of winning by trying separately, feeling like they are being pulled apart. The holistic approach is focused effort and simple disciplines, which lead to fulfilling results over a lifetime.

Challenge Yourself to Mastery

 Focus not on just one piece, but the bigger picture. If you're in doubt, simply ask for help. Put it up to your elevated reinforcements (your high-vibe tribe, God, The Universe, Angels, Guides, Nature, fate whoever or whatever that may be for you). You can ask a question in this way:

• "Please help me figure this out with the best possible outcome, thank you so much!"

Tammy Mastroberte shared how this works for her every time.

Sometimes she forgets to use it in the moment. One situation was when she was trying to help her cat and he was going crazy, she had been crawling under tables and trying to get him. Then she clicked and asked her high-vibe team, "Please anything you can do to help me in this situation? Thank you." Two minutes later the cat came and lay down in front of her.

Tammy is an Author and Spiritual Teacher, here spotting the signs and synchronicities. She shares her secrets for calling in Higher Help (Angels, Goddesses, Saints) for guidance and answers in any area of life.

Win Every Day

There is a saying that any day above ground is a good day. You can win every day by being the best person you can be too. When emotions are frustrating, you can go back to the foundational pieces of the success pyramid and start there, simply doing your best. This is living impactfully, living out your values. Living them out in your workplace, with your family and in your community. Don't keep it to one area, let that positive ripple effect flow. If you're a great athlete, be that in your communication too, don't go and be that nasty person to others. Rise beyond those traits and tendencies of hurting another in words or deeds, no excuses, we're going beyond that now.

I recall two key messages as I worked and travelled around the world when I was in my 20's:

• "Life isn't fair." I didn't think that it was very fair being told this whenever there was something causing me distress. It didn't seem helpful. The message: Use this as a reminder to make the most of everything you do have.

• "No excuses." There was no space to explain why a situation had occurred. It was what it was. The method of delivery seemed harsh. The message from this one: This is about your ability to accept what is. It is not good or bad, it just is.

We don't need to attach a story to it. What we can do is do our best, keep learning, growing and moving forward.

Politeness

Politeness and courteousness are a part of the bridge to success, but there is a caveat. Have awareness of our honesty and integrity in our communication.

How many times have you heard someone say they were just being "polite"? Often, what they really did was skip the truth. This also can translate into meaning they have lied a little. Why would they lie? The frequent answer is they did not want to hurt the other person's feelings. I've seen this in employment situations. This is not a win-win respectful interaction. You think you have helped them feel better, but left yourself still unable to express what could really help them 'be' better, either in your company, or in another.

What would you really like them to know that could make a positive difference?

Express yourself and share that pertinent information with them. You can be polite and courteous, as well as show vision and compassion.

How do I overcome this tendency to avoid saying the things that really do matter?

Pause and become aware of where you tend to do this. As mentioned, I have observed this in workplaces. The kinder way is to be honest and upfront in a thoughtful respectful manner.

This is where places like Toastmasters are worth their weight in gold. I recall initially not being that keen on attending the meetings. I knew it was a good idea to at least look and see what it was really like, firsthand. I spent a year within this community and learnt the ropes. I completed my ten speeches, among various other roles and received my competent communicator award. It added value to my communication and confidence.

The Sandwich Effect

The Toastmasters tip I like referring to as the "Sandwich Effect," is the first method recommended in many Toastmasters describing the "classic" sandwich technique for evaluations. It is polite, courteous and helpful.

• People let you know what you did well in your speech at the start, what they saw as your strengths.

• In the middle of the sandwich they provide information to you, suggesting where you could enhance certain areas. The language is using the word "and" rather than "but." The word "but" often negates the positive words spoken prior.

• This sandwich is finished with more good things they liked about your speech and what they saw as further strengths you were demonstrating. More of what you were doing well.

You are left feeling satisfied. You have some constructive points. You have further insights.

You can use this information well. There are some work ons to enhance your presentation. You've also received confidence in what you got right. You're not afraid to speak your mind in this way to another in the group as you will get that turn too.

If you were to eat this sandwich it would be nutritious, tasty and have a great effect on your mind, body and spirit. A win-win situation, fully expressed, kind, honest and helpful. Easy to do, yet many have got into the practise of it being easier not to do. This may feel like short term gains but can lead to long term losses with relationships suffering in the process. It can also be likened to eating something healthy or going for that unhealthy snack. If you are creating a sandwich, what are you putting into it. Some even forgo the bread and have lettuce as their outside crust.

Many people hate and avoid confrontation. When you communicate using these techniques it is not confrontation but communication and doing so in a way that empowers you both. It allows even those awkward messages to be shared. You demonstrate courage and in the long game you experience less conflict and upset. Your practice is one of doing this in a healthy front-footed way.

Practice this often, whether it be with your children, in business negotiations, or in tricky and awkward times. Utilise this skill. When important information for the good of the situation and all involved, is to be shared, remember it's wise to use it then.

At Toastmasters you get to see how you do come across to others. This includes feedback on your content, tone and body language. You get to find out what the audience perceives. You get to be the audience too. Participating as both teacher and student. Does what you say align well? Did your audience get the same message you were portraying? How did you think you were being? How did they feel it from their angle? How were you really coming across.

Some people have a resting face that gives off the impression they are angry, unapproachable people, when in fact they are not, or do not think they are. Having your default face with at least a little smile may benefit you and others greatly.

In psychology the third pane of "the Johari window" is the blind spot. This is the area others know of you, but you don't know of yourself. This could be another safe space to find them. You don't know what you don't know, so don't be afraid to shine the light of awareness on that part too.

The Johari window is explained further in the resources section of this book.

We're taking charge, making decisions; common sense is our common practice. You can't undo anything that happened yesterday. However, we have today, let's make the most of it. Our window of tolerance is increasing, our prefrontal cortex, that executive decision maker is online.

Your Big Goal in Life

Are you going to make a difference out there, being the best you that you can be?

Doing your best is a choice. If something got you down, you could still make the most out of your day. You have the gift of life. You can strive to influence people in the right way. You can seek out a different path with greater integrity. When trying in business, health and relationships, you can use foundational focused disciplines, simple efforts applied daily.

This is what highly regarded people and businesses practice. Challenge yourself to master these simple daily efforts. Then do so with more effortless ease and joy. Do this for a glimpse at your true potential. You are applying this without force, being vivid and strong. You have the gift of clarity. You are continuing and creating a legacy with wisdom and knowledge.

The path forward, my way is not the only right way. You have moved into a bigger unfolding of the holistic whole person approach to success. Its opposite was having a large impact and influence on us. You're now in the practice of going to your centre point of peace and unity. The more we take time each day to cultivate our inner peace and unity the more we can embrace the diversity of us all.

The Centre Point

Think of the middle point behind your belly button and ground yourself. This is the Dantian, or dan tian, energy centres in traditional Chinese Medicine (TCM). Translated from Chinese to mean "field of elixir." It describes what's believed by some to be the seat of life force energy in the body. Dantian are qi or energy flow centres in the body also referred to as Hara in Japanese.

It is a concept used in qigong, tai chi, and other Chinese martial arts. Central to Japanese acupuncture is the concept of Hara diagnosis, a diagnostic method that involves assessing the abdomen to gain insights into a patient's health. In Japanese culture, the Hara, is considered the body's centre of gravity and the seat of one's physical and spiritual well-being - our Core.

Where your attention goes, the energy flows. Your willingness and actions: You are allowing this better version to unfold. The hurt, destruction and distrust of the past no longer must continue. You are in your vehicle; you know your destination. You admire and look up to yourself and others.

Today and years from now you will appreciate building your character, integrity and team. Have the humble strength, industriousness and enthusiasm to steadily work well at life and love whatever you're doing.

As you study these philosophies that have been relevant for generations, you can see yourself being of greatness and goodness. Sometimes there can be pressure felt with certain words, as they trigger reminders of experiences, which were not so nice. There is now softness. Demonstrate the art of allowing, showing movement into your greatest self. Regardless of the words spoken notice your ability to become more at peace with it all.

"Sticks and stones may break my bones, but words do not hurt me." I remember this chant from our school playground when someone was being picked on. They did this as a way of saying I do not receive these nasty comments. It was a rhyme used as a defence against name calling and verbal bullying. I am not letting their cruel words hurt or affect my well-being.

Know that a sense of peace and serenity is with you. Sometimes it may feel too hard, too much hard work and not enough joy. In the past it seemed as if the rest of your life got put on hold. You would carry through with these goals only, but you can also find your centre, calmness, inner strength and resilience.

Who and Why

Who are you doing this for and why?

You are not here to put so much pressure on yourself, pretending you are doing it for others. When did you last check in with them and yourself about what you really do want? If you don't, you may become resentful and mean to others in your words and actions. You may burn out, or you can get a beautiful balance. Choose loving awareness and kind communication as your defaults.

The Story of Two Bright Students

After they left school, one student did not know what to do and went straight to the workforce to earn money. His parents were worried about him as he was regularly changing jobs. He showed no signs that University was in his sites, he didn't seem to know what he wanted to do. However, he was gaining a lot of work experience and getting to know his likes, dislikes and which fields of work he preferred.

The other student was attending University and achieving his degree. His parents were pleased. He was only doing this because he thought that it was what his parents and society expected of him, he eventually dropped out. He went out to the work force and got a job. At first, he was doing what seemed menial tasks, but he was bright, capable and was enjoying being there. With this newfound passion he moved through the ranks.

The moral to the story, decide what is right for you, don't follow someone else's dream, find yours. Study in the school of life. This can also be in the workplace, completing courses and certificates for your trade or going to university, explore and find what else may now be right for you.

Don't worry if it doesn't happen straight away, you're here to keep learning and growing anyway. Step up and put your best foot forward. You may as well explore and find out what you really do and don't like.

Both students in this story are finding their way, neither one better, nor worse than the other. They are still learning, still choosing, and making the most of the opportunities. It's more than okay if their dreams and desires change as they change, grow and evolve. In the meantime, they can keep giving of their best and keep choosing their way forward. They are not afraid to do something that may not be considered the norm. They know they can forge a new path that's right for them.

Warren Buffett said "It's better to hang out with people better than you. Pick out associates whose behaviour is better than yours and you'll drift in that direction."

May they be reading or hearing this now, smiling to themselves and saying: "Thanks, I like having that reminder, and yes I'm getting to do that too."

Warren Edward Buffett is an American investor and philanthropist who currently serves as the chairman and CEO of Berkshire Hathaway. As a result of his investment success, Buffett is one of the best-known investors in the world.

Check in regularly with not only yourself, but those people you care most about. Are you demonstrating the skills and habits as the role model you are and want to be?

Strengthening Relationships

This could be a weekly or even monthly exercise.

- Friends and family, from their perspectives:

Am I... being a good friend, mother, daughter, father, son to you?

How could I... be a better friend, mother, daughter, father, son for you?

- Workplace, from their perspective:

Am I ... doing a good job for you?

Is there ... anything else you need from me?

Then you know where you stand with them this week and you also know what you might choose to work on for the next week.

Just because you are not doing so well in an area doesn't mean it is not your strength or weakness; it just hasn't been your priority that week.

Very successful rounded lives, even with hours of dedicated training occurring are possible too. What the outsider may see as sacrifices for other family members to succeed can be switched to a team plan. With great communication, a shared vision, a greater level of joy and awareness can be reached together.

Working Smarter

How can you work so hard with all of this and have the quality of time elsewhere? Work smarter, not harder. "Work smarter, not harder," means to focus on being more efficient and effective in your work by finding ways to optimise your process and achieve results with less wasted time and energy, rather than simply putting in more hours or brute force effort.

What strategy and smart techniques can you implement to get things done better? This is not just by working longer or harder, but smarter, being more effective and efficient.

Often you can bring what can be perceived as negativity up and feel limited with options. This is frequently due to a trigger, a reminder of a past negative experience. In this instance let's create your team. I can be as small as you and one other, or as invisible seeming as you and the universe. If something feels too commercialised and focused on results at all costs, that simply may not be your path. If this or other undesirable situations are arising in your life, ask the question: "What is here for me to learn?" Write down your possible answers and strategies.

What if well-intentioned people are trying to enforce their beliefs and ways upon you?

We can become a little resistant if we feel pressured, or that we are being preached to, especially if that is not our wish or expectation of an interaction. You are a worthy powerful being, even if at times you may doubt this in yourself. This pressured, or pushy feeling is one many receive, when they are resisting at the same time. The person may then appear even pushier. Listen and hear, be firm, kind and clear. They sometimes need acknowledgement that you see, hear and appreciate them. This does not mean you have to follow where they may lead.

Pop into your power, listen, be the observer of you and the situation and choose your best way forward. When people are doing this in a way you feel is not respecting you, even if it is inadvertently, be mindful of your reaction to this and to them. Shelve that information, as sometimes it may simply not be right for you now. It could mean never, and your all-wise all-knowing self will keep you on track with that. This all wise all-knowing you can be found in your enquiry as you ask great questions, connect and become responsible for yourself and your actions.

There are many ways to travel to your destinations, and some ways work better for you than others. Notice your environment: it can be sustaining for one yet depleting for another. Some like lots of activity, others find it a distraction, some love the heat, and thrive whereas others feel like they shrivel and melt.

The Tale of the Mountain Lady

A lovely lady moved to the Mountains. Good mountain air one would think would be beneficial, and she loved to ski often. Spending a day on the ski field and living up there were totally different. The latter lead to overwhelm for her body. Soon after moving up there her skin broke out and she became rather ill.

The climate did not suit her body, and when she moved to a warmer flatter place, her skin cleared up and she felt much better.

Honouring the Way

When you meet with those who feel they are the only ones with "the" way, it can put you off, and you might go into your cave or choose to head for the mountains. Taking on too many external demands can lead to overwhelm. You may not feel good enough, because it's working for them, and not for you. What's wrong with you, they are so strong and confident in their belief, what are you doing wrong? Maybe reframe that question - what can you do that's right for you?

I recall a well known and loved teacher acting in this seemingly pushy manner, and I didn't like it. It did not feel honouring of people, and a lesson to learn from this is: "Where was the intent?" If the intent was kind, compassionate and being of service, maybe we need to see behind that veil of how it initially seemed to us.

Look for and even ask what the intent is. Begin again and hear the message from a higher place. Then do what feels like your next right step. Just like us they are learning too.

Choice

To handle any feelings of overwhelm remember you always have the freedom of choice. Even when it seems you are being pushed up against the wall with nowhere to go, you still get to choose how you want to feel about it. Regardless which country, religion or beliefs you hold, in that moment, ask for help, ask your elevated team, "please show me the way, the best way for me to handle this, I love you, I am listening, thank you." Now see what shows up.

The choice may be your attitude. In some circumstances it is perhaps the only thing you can really change. *As a Man Thinketh,* so is he - British author James Allen. This was first published in 1903 and is considered a self-help classic. His wife Lily Allen said: "He never wrote theories, or for the sake of writing; but he wrote when he had a message, and it became a message only when he had lived it out in his own life and knew that it was good."

James Allen (1864-1912) became famous for his inspirational writing. Allen's work influenced many self-help writers, including Dale Carnegie and Napoleon Hill.

Your Best

Who is the best you? Practice living this out even more.

You are here to give of your best. You are resilient. You do the right thing for the greatest good. This isn't just about me or you, it's the bigger picture, that "we," the interconnectedness of us.

"We are the world," standing together as one. The theme song for Live Aid in 1985 when Rock and Roll changed the world, a record 1.9 billion viewers tuned in to experience the charity concert. Approximately $63million was raised and ninety percent was sent to Africa. That was seen as the need then, the focus to feed those starving in Ethiopia and neighbouring Sudan. It showed how people can come together in the face of adversity and help their fellow man.

Fast forward to today, reflect on this event. It was a massive undertaking and not one that has been repeated. The faces of charitable giving and influence changed and increased. Even though discord in the world remained, there was a positive shift. Let's never underestimate your continued simple acts of daily kindness and doing your best.

You too are showing humanity the way forward. As you reflect on your appreciation and what you would like to see more of, more of a positive shift occurs.

You receive the lesson, you appreciate the experience, and you open the gift with thank you and I forgive you, and I forgive myself for not remembering. I am the love that I need, and we are all part of this.

Ho'oponopono

Another tool for handling overwhelm and bringing you back to your centre is the ancient Hawaiian practice "Ho'oponopono." It was designed for helping restore harmony within, and with others. Originally used as a form of alternative dispute resolution, a practice of reconciliation and forgiveness. It is a simple yet profound forgiveness practice that many found immediate benefits within their personal life.

Ho'oponopono:

• I'm sorry,

• Please forgive me,

• Thank you,

• I love you.

I love you. I'm sorry. Please forgive me. Thank you.

The other nice thing about the simplicity of repeating these four phrases is that practically all of us agree that those four concepts are valuable and important.

It then doesn't matter if the collective consciousness that Jung and many eastern traditions speak of occurs. If each culture was to tap into a level of awareness and focus of love, thanks, forgiveness, I'm sorry, what can now occur and come up to be cleared?

The Ho'oponopono technique is like the loving kindness intention. It's a practice to take you to a zero point, like using a rubber/eraser erasing all that has occurred which does not serve well. With this, you send the message of "I love you, I'm sorry, please forgive me, thank you" or "loving kindness." It could be as simple as repeating those 4 phrases or expanding it further to something like this: "I'm sorry for anything I, or my ancestors have thought, said, or done, that has caused any harm to anyone or anything anywhere. Please forgive me and them for knowingly, unknowingly, intentionally, unintentionally, consciously or unconsciously creating these issues and repeating these patterns that caused and created this challenge. Thank you for clearing and healing this, for me, my ancestors, my family, friends, anyone affected by this anywhere, including all future generations too. I love you for this process of making things right throughout all space, time and timelines."

In your mind, or out loud repeat and send these messages to yourself, someone you love, someone neutral and someone you have challenges with. For some it is tricky to say these words to those they have conflict, or ill feeling toward. Even though you are not doing it to their face and the other person has no idea, it can be a powerful tool to breakthrough and free yourself of the pain burden, angst and can even support resolution.

Let your inner disharmony be tuned to more harmonious ways.

You are all doing the best you know how, until you know better and do better.

To always walk one's talk can be a high expectation to place on another. Use these mental foundations, motivation, actionable strategies to empower you. You can choose to learn, grow, improve and thrive.

Hew Len

Dr. Hew Len was a student of Ho'oponopono and had worked at the Hawaii State Hospital in the high security ward for the criminally insane from 1983 to 1987. Many witnesses claim that Dr. Hew Len didn't do any therapy on the patients. He would walk through the ward, and review the patients' files, but not for the purpose of therapy.

Initially chaos reigned, it was a destructive depressive place with brawls every day, and staff often on sick leave. However, during that period, the inmates became less destructive and the mental ward employees made more initiative to make the ward a better place.

By the end, prisoners were released, and the staff performed their responsibilities dutifully again. Only a few inmates were left, and eventually, they were transferred to other wards. The clinic was closed.

When he was asked what caused the patients to change, his simple answer is always "I was simply healing the part of me that created them." He believed that total responsibility for your life means that everything in your life – simply because it is in your life – is your responsibility. In a literal sense the entire world is your creation. If you take complete responsibility for your life, then everything you see, hear, taste, touch, or in any way experience is your responsibility because it is in your life.

Family

 Your roles are changing. If you have children, they too grow up and want their freedom to fly high. How good can they be?

Your communication changes, it's from a new level of awareness, they are now adults you love and care about. Let them know you see them as strong, loving, kind, capable, resourceful and resilient people.

Let them know and sense this whether they are three or aged eighty-three.

If you don't quite feel that yet, ask them how you can be a better parent or friend to them? You want to see the best in them shine. If they are struggling a little you can still help them bring out their best. Do they know they are deeply loved and profoundly loveable? Letting them know that you are there for them and love them regardless. You're proud of them. This can sometimes be enough of a reminder for them to demonstrate that they too have got this and are more than okay. Notice their ability to show up as their next best version and notice your ability to do this too. Our children can be our greatest teachers.

Sometimes they're like a boomerang and keep coming back for more and at other times they're off doing their thing. The bottom line is you believe in them and show this in your thoughts, words and actions. They can sense and know this. You don't dictate or abdicate but communicate and allow them to make choices too. Practice these skills with them from their infancy or even start now. In the early years it's your time, support, care, guidance and encouragement that is required. All the way through it is your unconditional love. I see you. I hear you. I acknowledge you. I appreciate you and yes, I love you too.

You are a role model and continue to learn and be grateful for all life's gifts. Ideally your actions are those you would like your children to learn from of what to do, rather than what not to do.

I didn't find any one person that was doing all the things in the way I wanted to, but that did not mean I could not learn a lot from many and pave my own way. We all do this to some degree, sometimes you also learn from another of what not to do, so never think it was all for nothing nor be too hard on yourself.

What is right for you? What feels good on so many levels? Keep moving into more of this and feelings of overwhelm can diminish.

What are your ten loves? How often are you doing these?

Remind yourself what you did well today and decide what you want to do even better.

Repeat the phrase: "I am excited" out loud and see how long it takes you to feel the vibration of being excited. Play with this:

• "I am excited."

What exciting things are happening next?

Even if you don't believe it at first, say I'm excited out loud. It increases authentic feelings of excitement.

A Harvard Study published by the American Psychological Association found that affirmative statements like "I'm excited" helped people improve their performance compared to self-pep talks that urged relaxing statements such as "I am calm."

When people feel anxious and try to calm down, they are thinking about all the things that could go badly. When they are excited, they are thinking about how things could go "well."

"Champions keep playing until they get it right" Billie Jean King.

Billie Jean King is famous for her tennis career and her advocacy for women's rights. She fought for equal pay for women in tennis, women's rights in sports, and LGBTQ+ rights. She is considered one of the greatest tennis players of all time, winning 39 Grand Slam titles, including 20 at Wimbledon. She was the world's top-ranked women's tennis player for six years between 1966 and 1975. King also defeated Bobby Riggs in the 1973 "Battle of the Sexes" tennis match, which was the most-watched tennis match ever at the time. The match brought attention to women's pay equality in sports.

Whatever your gender identity is, you are a great person, notice this. There are many great people around you, lean in, give of your best, believe in your greater good and cheer one another on.

Remember it's all okay. You're in the right place at the right time.

CHAPTER 12: BEYOND MONEY

"I attribute my success to this: I never gave or took any excuse."
Florence Nightingale

Florence Nightingale (1820-1910) is famous for establishing the standards of modern nursing and for her work to improve hospital hygiene and safety. She is also known as "The Lady with the Lamp" for carrying a lamp to see her patients at night. In 1854, Nightingale led a team of nurses to care for British soldiers in the Crimean War. She was shocked by the poor conditions at the military hospital in Scutari, Turkey, and worked to improve hygiene and cleanliness. Nightingale is considered the founder of modern nursing. In 1860, she established the world's first nursing school at St. Thomas Hospital in London. Nightingale was a statistician who used data to understand how the world worked. She created one of the first pie charts. She used a "rose diagram" to show how the death toll from disease fell after the Sanitary Commission's work.

The Thirty Day Exercise

Move into the fullness of the joy, creativity and magnificence. Not giving or taking any excuse, what do you feel you need to do to achieve this?

• Imagine for one minute I was to hand over a million dollars to you, what would you do with it?

• Here's a million more. Imagine for another minute what else can now be done?

• Just for good measure here's 20 billion dollars, so take a few more minutes to take this in. Are you getting the picture? What can you now do?

• Dream big, bigger, self, local to global, no boundaries, no limits.

At this stage of your journey your job is to get your creative juices flowing, no barriers, you are free to fly, nothing is impossible. No time to pause to judge your thoughts, just write, think of what else could be done. Visualise, let anything that excites and inspires you transport you into a world of new possibility, and write, or even draw more.

What would/could make a positive difference to you and others? Regardless of how impossible it may currently seem - yes dare to dream and ignite a light in you. Go forward into this some more, igniting your dreams and desires, perhaps even finding a vision, idea, or ambition, that may have been hidden for a very long time.

Try this exercise for at least five minutes every day for the next thirty days and see what actions you are taking by day thirty-one.

What would you do? Where would that money go, to what, to whom, what would you like to see, how would you like the world to be?

You have the power, write this out. As you play here start to get clear and every time any doubt comes up, go into your solution box where answers for the greatest good and divine guidance reside. A space where there is no harm to you or others, to serve and be of service, going beyond.

I would love to see everyone's stories and visions of how great things can be. Our collective vision and our allowing of this or something even better working out. Us co-creating and interacting with harmony and peace. What bliss and prosperity can we now achieve?

Now that you've got more clarity let's break it down.

• Each day: Do one thing each day towards that vision.

You are here to create this, or something even better. You don't lose motivation; you just don't revisit your mission and vision often enough.

It starts with us, each one of us. You are no longer dwelling in the problems and the blame game of the past but envisioning and creating your fantastic future now. What are the commonalities, how can you come together to collaborate and create more of this?

There are groups, community, adventures to join in on, or create them for yourself. You can be in the vortex of uplifting one another right here, right now.

Money

You are going beyond money now. How does one do that? Money is another form of energy and has been your dominant means of exchange. There are higher vibrations of divine and unconditional love for us to be playing in now too. Your attachment to money lessens, your accumulation of more moves to your abundant life and gifts you possess.

You can release your hold on money and its hold on you. Let us serve each other well. You are allowing better into your life in its many forms. What is beyond the form of money and how your relationship has been with it? What else is here for you?

You can release old paradigms. What you put in your mind, your body and through your movement. What is now part of the amazing triangle and web you weave? You can still have more than enough; you simply see the bigger picture. Money is a man-made measure and a part of the full equation.

Money is valuable because everyone knows everyone else will accept it as a form of payment. At first our currency was believed to be a barter system and then easily traded goods like animal skins, salt and weapons developed over the centuries. Barter and trade were the exchange. China was the first country to use recognisable coins, but the first minted coins were created not too far away in Lydia (now Western Turkey). I didn't know that when I backpacked through Turkey in the early '90s. It was a fascinating country to explore, and at that time, it was renowned for its well-priced gold and silver. We purchased this with another form of currency, exchanging our traveller's cheques for Turkish Liras and lovely jewellery was ours.

I heard a powerful comment about the phrase "money doesn't buy you happiness" the reply was "you either haven't given enough away, or you haven't earned enough."

Some people get rather concerned about their money situation. If this is you too, use your pain or discomfort, don't let it use you. Turn any minor setback into a major comeback. Adjust and pivot, don't let this stop you, become unstoppable. If you're struggling in any area, use that struggle to make you stronger from today.

Good Emotions

There's a spectrum of emotions for releasing beneficial neuropeptides and feeling better. Get yourself into a good feeling zone, so you make choices that honour who you are and what you are desiring.

Listen to, say and write out these words:

- Acceptance.
- Courage.
- Passion, Desire.
- Inspiration, Creativity.
- Self-Esteem.
- Pride, Fulfilment.
- Willingness.

- Co-operation, Belonging.

- Peace, Serenity.

- Happiness.

- Love.

- Unconditional love, Altruism.

- Faith, Trust.

- Gratitude.

- Joy and Ecstasy.

Now demonstrate these words by your actions. Create more abundance in your life with the deep knowing that abundance is waiting to meet you too.

What if there are a few missing pieces. What are you overlooking?

There are 24 hrs in a day, how are you interacting with these hours in your day? Bring your meditation and mindfulness to life and live it as you breathe, your breath is your source. This goes way beyond money and fears you may have.

Let's check in regularly. Are you coming from the space of that loving kind abundant magnificent self that is within us all? No worries if you aren't or haven't been and you are being hard on yourself right now. What is your intent? Start there.

You are here to "be love," to "be understanding," rather than be loved and understood. It must come from you first.

Our messages now and messages thirty years ago on this level are almost the same. The key difference is an openness and willingness by many more is here now. There is a deeper level of awareness upon us to invite in.

There's technology that brings us together with an abundance of information, connecting us across the world. According to an article "Digital in 2017 Global Overview" the report revealed that more than half of the world now uses the internet. Almost two thirds of the world's population have a mobile phone, and it was only twenty-five years ago that World Wide Web was available to the public.

What can you now create that you thought was previously impossible. You're not here to be realistic, you're courageous.

Please no matter how right you think your way is, listen to others with love and compassion and find the common threads that unite you.

People reply that they understood, "very good and very true," so how do we move people from the understanding of "in word form" to understanding from "living this truth form? Here are some answers from the universe:

When life seems draining rather than life giving and life enhancing, it's time to change things up a little. You've shifted, but you stayed in your same old ways, instead of shifting into your new lighter space that has opened for you.

Others may be more experienced than you in different areas, but no-one is better or lesser than you. Yes, some of their actions may have been, but you have your gifts and life lessons to learn. If the seemingly unbalanced hierarchy irritated you, you no longer must feed that system or put your attention to that which you do not want more of.

Where your intention and action go your energy flows.

In times of change it may initially feel restrictive, and you can even feel a bit critical. You might veer back and forth to change and then not want to because it's uncharted ground. Your critical voice might talk louder to you, and you find yourself being mean to yourself, or thinking cruelly of others.

Often as we seek to go beyond money, we find we have more than enough.

The gentleman who was looking for a partner stopped looking. He focused on being a better person himself, appreciating what he did have, and the partner showed up.

The job hunter needed money, so they did what they could to be a great employee. They boldly offered their services for free and other paid offers showed up.

This is about going beyond money. These people didn't necessarily have what they wanted show up straight away.

- Did they nearly give up? Yes.
- Did they have times of doubt and uncertainty? Yes.
- During this time did they feel like it was taking too long? Yes.
- Did they choose to work smarter and review their spending habits? Yes.
- Did they look at other options and opportunities they'd never explored before? Yes.
- Did they believe it was still going to work out well? Yes.

And what if you could do this all so much quicker and easier? Hold that space and trust that it will work out well and it will. Sometimes it's just not as you may have expected it.

As you reflect on your life's work and the lessons you have learned, tap into the infinite, as you are already much better than you think you are.

Practical Money Tips

As you tap into your ability to see and go beyond money, you may want some practical tips to help you out now. I have created various surveys, quizzes and reflection tests. Here are some questions and points from within the Releasing Financial Stress test.

• Create a spreadsheet or piece of paper with labels to evaluate where you are at and what you are choosing to spend your money on, e.g. Income, bills, groceries, entertainment, car, purchases. I have groceries under the label food, and I also have a food discretionary category too.

Monitor, measure and review.

We used to do this every couple of months. Now we find doing this every month works even better. It gives us a good finger on the pulse of where we are spending our money. This means we can course correct if needed. At the end of the year, we will evaluate our income and expenditure and 'know our numbers'. This gives us the knowledge of how much it costs us to live, what our fixed costs are, our discretionary costs and what ways we can improve.

Where can you reduce spending or increase wealth?

• The highest version of you. Does your spending match this financial freedom you desire? You are changing and evolving, are your spending habits evolving too? Visualise and describe how you would like this to be as if it already was your reality now.

• What habits and skills can you now put in place towards this more abundant you? This could be simple disciplines like reducing and clearing debt, including credit cards. Opening a savings account and putting part of your income there each week. Set fun goals, short, medium and long.

• How can you enjoy what you are doing even more? You may start a "side hustle" (creating a new source of income without quitting your day job) and transition into something you are passionate about.

When I was working in the financial services industry it was about starting something small and making progress. The earlier you started the less you needed to put aside as you could take advantage of the compounding interest effect. It wasn't the amount that counted, but the disciplined regular and consistent approach, the plan. The saying was: "If you fail to plan, you are planning to fail."

Rather than saying: "If I had more money I would have a better plan," have a better plan to have more money. The model was to pay yourself first. The key was not only how to spend it, but what to spend it on and for. This is determined by your personal philosophy. A good philosophy for financial independence and wealth for the future is to start early and small. It's much harder to automatically put aside $100,000 of your $1,000,000 than it is 10 cents of your $1.

The message: The way to success is to get started.

See the resources section for other books, quizzes and tests that are available for you.

Ten Top Money Tips

From Billionaire Investor and Philanthropist Warren Buffet:

1. Reinvest Your Profits

When you first make money, you may be tempted to spend it. Don't. Instead, reinvest the profits. Buffett learned this early on. In high school, he and a pal bought a pinball machine to put in a barbershop. With the money they earned, they bought more machines until they had eight in different shops. When the friends sold the venture, Buffett used the proceeds to buy stocks and to start another small business.

2. Be Willing to Be Different

Don't base your decisions upon what everyone is saying or doing. When Buffett began managing money in 1956 with $100,000 cobbled together from a handful of investors, he was dubbed an oddball. He worked in Omaha, not on Wall Street, and he refused to tell his partners where he was putting their money. People predicted that he'd fail, but when he closed his partnership 14 years later, it was worth more than $100 million.

3. Never Suck Your Thumb

Gather in advance any information you need to make a decision and ask a friend or relative to make sure that you stick to a deadline. Buffett prides himself on swiftly making up his mind and acting on it. He calls any unnecessary sitting and thinking "thumb-sucking."

4. Spell Out the Deal Before You Start

Your bargaining leverage is always greatest before you begin a job – that's when you have something to offer that the other party wants. Buffett learned this lesson the hard way as a kid, when his grandfather Ernest hired him and a friend to dig out the family grocery store after a blizzard. The boys spent five hours shovelling until they could barely straighten their frozen hands. Afterward, his grandfather gave the pair less than 90 cents to split.

5. Watch Small Expenses

Buffett invests in businesses run by managers who obsess over the tiniest costs. He once acquired a company whose owner counted the sheets in rolls of 500-sheet toilet paper to see if he was being cheated (he was). He also admired a friend who painted only the side of his office building that faced the road.

6. Limit What You Borrow

Buffett has never borrowed a significant amount — not to invest, not for a mortgage. He has gotten many heart-rending letters from people who thought their borrowing was manageable but became overwhelmed by debt. His advice: Negotiate with creditors to pay what you can. Then, when you're debt-free, work on saving some money that you can use to invest.

7. Be Persistent

With tenacity and ingenuity, you can win against a more established competitor. Buffett acquired the Nebraska Furniture

Mart in 1983 because he liked the way its founder, Rose Blumkin, did business. A Russian immigrant, she built the mart from a pawnshop into the largest furniture store in North America. Her strategy was to undersell the big shots, and she was a merciless negotiator.

8. Know When to Quit

Once, when Buffett was a teen, he went to the racetrack. He bet on a race and lost. To recoup his funds, he bet on another race. He lost again, leaving him with close to nothing. He felt sick — he had squandered nearly a week's earnings. Buffett never repeated that mistake.

9. Assess the Risks

In 1995, the employer of Buffett's son, Howie, was accused by the FBI of price-fixing. Buffett advised Howie to imagine the worst- and best-case scenarios if he stayed with the company. His son quickly realised that the risks of staying far outweighed any potential gains, and he quit the next day.

10. Know What Success Really Means

Despite his wealth, Buffett does not measure success by dollars. In 2006, he pledged to give away almost his entire fortune to charities, primarily the Bill and Melinda Gates Foundation. He's adamant about not funding monuments to himself-no Warren Buffett buildings or halls. "When you get to my age, you'll measure your success in life by how many of the people you want to have love you do love you. That's the ultimate test of how you've lived your life."

Wealth: Living a Rich Life

You may not aspire to have the money Warren Buffet accumulated, but even he did not measure his success by dollars. Life is much bigger than that. It also doesn't mean you must be a merciless negotiator or take shortcuts and become obsessive to live your rich life. There is the middle-way approach, which emphasises dialogue and peaceful negotiations. May you be in your power finding that happy medium and a win-win. May you also feel satisfied, fostering collaboration and long-term success, no longer with one party winning at the expense of others. Let's prosper together.

Enjoy your success beyond money. The meaningful relationships, personal fulfilment, positive impact on others, good health and well-being, a sense of purpose, continuous learning and growth, achieving personal goals, are some of what creates a successful rich life.

Be mindful: If we focus solely on accumulating money, we may miss out on experiencing a full, rich, and meaningful life.

Know Your Numbers

There is a saying that you can manage what you measure. What this means is you can improve something by tracking its progress. If you want to manage your money better, know where you spend it.

Know what you spend on an average, week, month, year.

- How much do you need and why?
- What do you want to do and get?
- What does it take for you to have your rich life?

One lady after reflecting on this was able to drop her work week to 4 days. Another at another stage in her life dropped to 1 and a half days. Another gentleman took early retirement. They realised they didn't need to wait to live the life they love.

Do you need to stay in the work and work place you are in? Do you need to keep doing the hours you are doing? If it's just because of the money, look again. What line of work do you enjoy? Know your numbers. Clear that debt. Leverage: This could mean getting income from assets you have, renting a home or a room, getting in a border. We loved being a homestay for international students especially when the children were young. We got to meet people from all around the world. Don't give up, instead explore some more. Put in some healthy boundaries and deadlines to achieve your goals. Review your fixed and discretionary spend. Look at some other options and ways that could be even better.

The List

Start a list exploring your current skills and expertise. If you need more convincing, on your abilities, think of all the daily things you do and have done. The interactions you have, the courses, the trainings, the experiences that have shaped you, the knowledge you have gained, the insights, the travel, the people, the new understandings. There are many new skills and expertise that you have and can attain.

All you are doing is adding to your value and competencies. This means you can reflect on the big and small achievements and challenges throughout your life so far. This could be where you find you can add value to another. Your value can create a positive exchange with one or many. You can achieve even more than you bargained for more effortlessly and joyfully. You get to choose.

Meeting Halfway

"What you need to know comes to you," but you've got to ask for it, recognise it and meet it halfway.

One lovely lady, who knows and believes that too, taps into this daily. What she needs to know comes to her. She uses this ability for the greatest good and well-being of her and her clients. She also does want to study and learn more. When you notice you have great wisdom coming through you, you can also be keen to understand it at another level. She honours that gift and feels it a privilege. For her having that in depth knowledge and deeper understanding brings greater self-satisfaction. The message is: if you want to study, then study, don't let your current belief systems around, study, work, money, age, stop you. If you don't want to take that path, there are many other ways to learn, grow and evolve. Release judgements on yourself and others. You can do amazingly either way. It is time to be true to your own heart.

• What is your motivation and the motives behind your choices?

• Does it excite you?

It's okay if you feel some trepidation. If the bigger picture is for life expanding, loving, kind, fascinating fun, you are most certainly on the right track.

For those that are bedridden, there is power of love and thought from your bedside, so never underestimate your power wherever you are.

Being Awake Aware Amazing

Awake, Aware and Amazing the 3 A's. When many of us started out in school it was the three r's reading, writing, and arithmetic. Times are changing and this integration and embracing is not only of accepting and embracing diversity in ourselves, but in others too. It is going beyond all this noise to the understanding and welcoming of our unity. At school you may have been taught or told to reach out a hand of friendship. We are now awakening our awareness and amazingness, and it's time for many hands of friendship to unite and break down the barriers and walls we have built of being afraid of one another.

Currently, we may not be able to hear, see, or smell what those in the animal kingdom can, but we do have the ability to discern.

Bees and birds can see ultraviolet light, which we humans can't. But we can see and sense danger. Dolphins and some fish can hear frequencies above 200,000 hertz. Us humans can generally hear sounds ranging from 20 hertz (Hz) to 20,000 Hz. Elephants and whales communicate using lower frequencies than we can detect. Yet we do have a field of intelligence we can tap into and expand our capabilities and unite.

We have galaxies as old as 13.2 billion years and the observable universe is estimated to contain more than 2 trillion galaxies. That sure opens things up for what else is available for us.

Fast forward to now, to our little place in the world. I grew up in a remote part of New Zealand where billions of stars were visible in the night sky. Not that I was counting or had that awareness back then how special a sight that was to see. Now light pollution means you must live remotely which many do not or go to places like Tekapo in New Zealand and pay to see the stunning night sky. This used to be available to virtually all of us everywhere in the world for free. Tekapo is a very special experience, and it is more than seeing the stars and galaxies with the naked eye, even the views from up there by day are beautiful.

When you realise that something is a rare sight to see, you appreciate it even more. What if everything you see is a rare sight to see? No one sees things exactly as you do. Your experiences colour your vision. How awake and aware are you to see the true magnificence of what is not only around, but within you.

Religion: Embracing our Differences and Similarities

Religion can be a tricky subject for many as it has seen more than its share of separation, war, anger and hypocrisy around it. We are not here to lord it over one another and feel our way our God is the only true God or religion. We are also not here to preach do as I say, not as I do. You're here to be a decent, kind person. Despite their differences, most religions share common elements like a belief in a higher power, a set of moral values, sacred rituals, the concept of a spiritual reality beyond human experience, and often, a focus on promoting peace and ethical behaviour, sometimes encapsulated by that golden rule of treating others as you would like to be treated.

When I travelled to Israel and through the West bank

our bus was full of bullet holes. Jerusalem and Bethlehem were fascinating, but still dangerous with demonstrations and shootings occurring.

I felt grateful for the experience and to meet wonderful people and to survive it well. The hearts and minds of many whether religious or not were being ruled by separation, suppression and fear. People felt cornered that there was no way out, they reacted from that part of them when there was so much more.

Now tides have turned. What if it is the age of acceptance, embracing and integrating all of ourselves inside and out, the earth, water, air, and fire? How could this look? We are going beyond what has been before.

Many people have feared Islam. In Sri Lanka we met a beautiful man whose faith was Islam. His message was one of kindness. He told us his religion was kindness. There are a lot of kind people out there, start looking for more of these aspects in others.

Leading from Your Heart

What happened in your past that closed your heart? Did you feel that if you were led by that, you would just get trampled on, perhaps used and abused?

Leading from your heart doesn't mean you don't have a voice. It also doesn't mean that when your voice does speak up it's one of anger and causes violence and arguments. That is not us, or your way forward.

There have been some deep ancestral wounds that you may not realise you are living and bringing into your future. You can love, learn and cut the ties that have held you back. Embrace and appreciate where things have been and use it as a springboard to where you are going.

You are in the time to shine. Yes, there is disruption, and even a bit of chaos. Be aware, you may tend to block yourself without even knowing it and creating a future that you don't really want to endure in the process.

• Check in. What are you thinking about, talking about and doing?

Take responsibility and not the blame game. Use everything that comes into your life as leverage to make yourself an even better version of the most amazing, powerful, loving, kind, wise and wonderful you.

Loving, enjoying, appreciating, working on these muscles, strengthen them and then as Michael Jackson said; "If you want to make the world a better place, take a look at yourself and make a change."

"Heal the world" was the song. Make it a song in action.

As you make this a song in action, notice how you can move beyond money and perhaps move into a life of ecstasy. "Heal your world."

Allow more good things from many spheres, so you are rich in the life you are creating. What does 'be rich' really mean? The book *You Were Born Rich* wasn't about money but the richness within you. You are already whole and complete, but you may have forgotten this and acted out in another way.

"Twenty years from now you will be more disappointed by the things that you didn't do than by the ones you did do, so throw off the bowlines, sail away from safe harbour, catch the trade winds in your sails. Explore, Dream, Discover" Mark Twain.

Mark Twain is best remembered for his two classic novels of boyhood life on the Mississippi River. His childhood home of Hannibal, Missouri, inspired many of his literary creations.

Disappointment and Missing Out

Street Life Story

There was a beggar on the streets, he was offered some woollen gloves as the weather was bitterly cold. He did not want them and said "no." He was then offered a woollen hat. He felt his cap was good enough. The beggar wanted money instead to buy his cigarettes. He did not receive the money. He also missed out on all the other gifts that were offered to him.

We wish to inspire people into their independence not support the habits that can do more harm. If you want to experience abundance, wealth, joy, what can you do to help other people to experience this? There is a saying that you keep what you give away. Intention, focus, and energy given is received back to you.

Mark Twain supposedly also coined the phrase: "Sing like no one is listening, love like you've never been hurt, dance like no one is watching, and live like it is heaven on earth." The dance of life, live without excuses.

Remember it's all okay. You're in the right place at the right time.

CHAPTER 13: YOUR INNER POWER AND GREATNESS

"If you want to awaken all of humanity, then awaken all of yourself, if you want to eliminate the suffering in the world, then eliminate all that is dark and negative in yourself. Truly, the greatest gift you have to give is that of your own self-transformation." Lao Tzu

Lao Tzu's literal meaning is "Old Master". Born in 571 BC, he was a Chinese philosopher, the author of the Tao Te Ching, and credited with founding the philosophical system of Taoism. The emphasis being harmony on the road, pathway.

Discover your inner power, the source of strength peace and purity within you.

Being successful in the past often meant abandoning health and healthy relationships. This is not what you are choosing for your present and future. There is no need to sacrifice to have success anymore.

You can have money, health and happiness, you can have it all. This is what is natural, but we have lost our focus.

You no longer must struggle, resist or sacrifice, but instead choose to move forward with the intent of being here to thrive.

It is no longer an either or. You have stepped into the power of having it all in life. If you are experiencing financial stress, and not as successful as you want to be, remember you can get out of this stressed, out of joy, unbalanced feeling.

You can change your job, break the cycle, reclaim your power. You can implement some new better habits and practices. You can use other appropriate tips, tools and techniques.

10 Keys

Here is more inspired thought and activity for you to play with as you enhance and enjoy many more moments:

- •1. If this moment did not feel that enhanced or great, while you're on this planet as a living breathing human being, you've got the next to redeem yourself.

- •2. Never feel you are not capable or good enough. You are far more than this.

- •3. Be loving, kind and patient with yourself, and smell the roses on your way, as you might have missed them in your hurry to get there, wherever your "there" is.

- •4. The comparison game is no longer the one you have yourself as second best. It's how you were to how you are now being.

- •5. You can always learn more. Gain the habits, skills and tools required to excel in the areas that are important to you.

- •6. Inspirational guidance is here for you to step into more and more. You can notice the synchronicity of people and events.

- •7. You can notice yourself taking more inspired action, no longer leaving it to chance. You are in action, alive and inspiring.

- •8. Your action, habit and skill accrual, finds you becoming more competent, eloquent, capable and masterful in the areas you choose.

- •9. You are safe in the knowledge that with your willing participation in this, this or something even better is working out. It will, it does, and so it is.

- •10. You are feeling so very grateful and empowered.

I looked at some work I did, articles I put into a scrap book in the 1980's when I was 16. There were tips and tools, just like the ones that are here for you now and I noticed this:

• Having incorporated the top level of what they suggested, yes, yoga was in the mix then too, I realised we cannot just do that top surface level and think, yep, my life is set, a long and healthy, stress-free existence.

• When you take your foot off the gas, and turn the car off, the car stops and so do you. Keep going deeper, it never ends and enjoy the rewards of this endless opening that lies before you.

• Do not stop here and think, ' Yes, I get it.' Turn that "I get it" into "I live it." You are living it out. You are unlocking more of your ability to thrive in life. If there's anything to stop, it's to stop restricting your awesomeness.

Observe the different aspects of us: the adult self, the adolescent self, and the child self. Integrate these qualities of wise, experienced, sweet, kind, loving and curious. Let them shine together and be the powerful you. Watch your world open one moment at a time. You are so loved, so appreciated and you too have invisible wings to fly and soar.

It doesn't matter what age or stage in life you are; you can begin with childlike wonder into the positive possibilities that await you now. Let your creative juices keep flowing into action and movement, freeing up blocks of the past.

Try out the tools in this toolkit and book. Use the keys and unlock your doors to more freedom and joy. Let your life unfold in your paradise one beautiful, fascinating, intriguing, fulfilling day at a time. If you feel like you're dropping back, or it's not working out, keep returning for insight, lean in and know you can be more than alright. **F**ace **e**verything **a**nd **r**ise, because you have got this, and you can feel great.

You breathe in thanks; you breathe out love. You breathe in light;

you breathe out joy - and so it is and can be.

Keep surrendering to your highest good and highest self. Stay within your centre and know you are grounded and strong. These are your earth-like qualities. Yet you are light and flexible, these are your star-like qualities.

You have released your idea of how things should be and opened to how good they can be. Enjoy this way of being.

Open into your own direct connection with inspiration.

Stay grounded and centred and inspiration can enter. You are anchoring in your heart and unfolding like a flower blooming.

Exercising Your Intuition

• Decide on something showing up, maybe a red balloon, a Dalmatian dog, something of your choosing. Keep it open, be aware and when you do see it in the next 48hrs, receive this as your reminder. This is your reminder that you are connected to something bigger. You have more abilities to explore and can play with this even more. If it takes longer, your patience and belief is simply being tested.

Your intuition, that inner intelligence and wisdom is the space to tune in to even more.

Thank you, thank you, thank you. Thank you so much for being here now.

You can grow without the pressure of before. Each time life strikes a chord for a new vibration return to this book and as you do notice your ability to understand at a deeper level and thrive even more.

Remember it is all okay. You are in the right place at the right time, every time. You are seen, heard and valued more than you can imagine. You have the keys, use them well.

Love Robyn X

APPENDIX A: USEFUL RESOURCES

There are so many resources to choose from so it's my pleasure in listing some that I have found useful over the years. May they support and inspire you into more of your greatness too:

• "Latest research suggests you have influence of over 95% of your well-being." Refer to Deepak Chopra. MD and The Chopra Center.

• The Johari window. This is a technique that helps people better understand their relationships with themselves and others.

The third pane was the Blind spot, the area others know of you, but you don't know of yourself.

The other panes are:

Open, traits that both yourself and others can perceive.

Hidden, or facade, traits you know, but others are unaware of in you.

Unknown, neither party realises.

• A great resource for personalised health is ph360. They have an online app called Shae that calculates personalised health advice just for you. Their website is ph360.me and they have a simple health type test you can do for free and receive a 15-page report, to assist you on your journey. The biotypes they refer to are - Sensor, Crusader, Activator, Guardian, Connector and Diplomat. It's at https://healthtype.ph360.me/test

• EWG Environmental Working Group: Information of products and ingredients.

• TM Transcendental Meditation. One of my current favourite

sites is through the David Lynch Foundation. Bob Roth does a fantastic job of Global Group meditations which I link into. There are many beautiful resources here: https://tm-meditate.org

The TM global link is: https://tm.org

For the Transcendental Meditation peer reviewed published studies conducted at a wide range of independent research institutions: https://research.miu.edu/tm-technique

Here in New Zealand two of the main sites to explore including accessing the free introductory talks: https://tm.org.nz and https://tmforwomen.co.nz

• I also hold Group Meditations at my home, in-person and online. Reach out to me if you would like to be included: keystofreedom1@gmail.com

• Heartmath Institute: This Institute researches and develops reliable scientifically based tools to bridge the heart mind connection.

• The 5 Love languages: Dr. Gary Chapman. A free online quiz is available to identify yours.1-Words of Affirmation.2-Quality Time.3-Receiving Gifts.4-Acts of Service.5-Physical Touch. http://www.5lovelanguages.com/profile/

• The 4 tendencies: Gretchen Rubin. Gretchen has a free quiz to identify your tendency. 1-Upholder.2-Questioner.3-Obliger.4-Rebel.https://www.surveygizmo.com/s3/4232520/gretchenrubinfourtendenciesquiz

• Robyn Hodge Coaching (Me). I have co-created *Keys to Freedom Journal*, The *Keys to Freedom Inspirational, Motivational & Gratitude* Quote Card Sets. Surveys/tests/quizzes/meditations are also available for free by request. https://robynhodgecoaching.com/contact/ There are some other tools available through https://robynhodgecoaching.com/resources/

Currently the best spot to make contact and explore more is via my calendly link:

https://calendly.com/robynhodgecoaching/keys

The surveys/tests/quizzes/meditations include:

1. Wellbeing, Mind, Body, Soul:

• For Your Wellbeing. A Holistic Health Review • Wellbeing. Nutrition Review • The Weekly Happiness Scale.

2. Review, Reflect, Reassess:

• At a Glance Update. Progress Check for You • Personal Stock-take. It's Time to Shine • The Litmus Test. Reviewing Your Priorities.

3. Business, Career, Finances:

• Releasing Financial Stress Test • Business Planning. Vision and Action Steps • Business Planning. Attraction and Retention • Into Your Excellence. Finding Yours • Identifying and Pursuing Your Passions.

4. Coaching, Workshops:

• Reflections. In a Great State • Coaching Satisfaction.

5. Meditation Series:

Meditations: • 5 minutes or under • 10 minutes • 20 minutes.

Some of the Books Mentioned in this Book:

- *You Can Heal Your Life* by Louise Hay. This has a symptoms list and the meanings behind it.

- *Man's Search for Meaning* by Viktor Frankl.

- *As a Man Thinketh* by James Allen.

Other Impactful Books, Authors, Sites:

Eat   to   Live   and   *Eat   For   Life.*   Books   by   Dr.

Joel Fuhrman.https://www.drfuhrman.com/blog/164/5-ways-to-amp-up-your-nutrient-intake

Food Revolution Network.
Science Based Nutrition for Life. Healthy Ethical Sustainable.
https://foodrevolution.org/

The Game Changers Movie. About plant-based eating, protein, and strength. Presented by James Cameron, Arnold Schwarzenegger, Jackie Chan.
https://gamechangersmovie.com

Pam Gregory UK Astrologer.
Pam has been involved with astrology for 45 years. It is her passion to help people. She sees astrology as a profound and sacred language of geometry and meaning that helps us to see the bigger picture. Her interest lies in seeing astrology in the context of our spiritual journey, and how new astrological discoveries are expanding our view of our life on Earth. https://www.youtube.com/@PamGregoryOfficial

Raising Your Spirited Child Workbook by Mary Sheedy Kurcinka. Techniques to help your child "hear" your message, plans for calming activities, tips for winning your child's cooperation, how to deal with mealtimes, bedtimes and meltdowns.

A Woman's Best Medicine by Nancy Lonsdorf M.D., Veronica Butler M.D., and Melanie Brown, PH.D. Health, happiness and long life through Maharishi Ayur-Veda.

One of the first Deepak Chopra books I read was *Perfect Health*. The Complete Mind/Body Guide. He has written many more.

One of the first Esther and Jerry Hicks book I read was *Ask and It Is Given*. Learning to Manifest Your Desires. They too have written many more.

Nutrition and Physical Degeneration by Weston A Price. A comparison of primitive and modern diets and their effects.

What your Doctor May Not Tell You About Menopause by Dr John R Lee M.D. He was a medical expert and pioneer in the use of natural progesterone cream, and this was a breakthrough book on Natural Hormone Balance.

The first book I read through Credence Publications and the series of books that are part of the CTM Campaign for Truth in Medicine was *Health Wars* by Phillip Day. They too have written many more.

I Quit Sugar for Life by Sarah Wilson. Your Fad-Free Wholefood Wellness Code and Cookbook.

Rich Dad Poor Dad by Robert T Kiyosaki and Sharon L Lechter. What The Rich Teach Their Kids About Money - That the Poor and Middle Class Do Not.

The Motivation Manifesto by Brendon Burchard. 9 Declarations to Claim Your Personal Power.

High Performance Habits by Brendon Burchard. 1-Seeking Clarity. 2-Generating Energy. 3-Raising Necessity. 4-Increasing Productivity. 5-Developing Influence. 6-Demonstrating Courage.

Research:

PubMed is a free resource and library of scientific literature. "Supporting the search and retrieval of biomedical and life sciences. It has the aim of improving health both globally and personally. Compromising of more than 37 million citations." https://pubmed.ncbi.nlm.nih.gov/

PubMed Central PMC is a free archive of biomedical and life sciences journal literature. It's part of the National Library of Medicine at the National Institutes of Health (NIH) (.gov). The link for (PMC) is https://pmc.ncbi.nlm.nih.gov/

Currently some of the most highly regarded scientific journals are: Nature, Science, The Lancet, and New England Journal of

Medicine.

Bristol Stool Chart:

Developed at the Bristol Royal Infirmary as a clinical assessment tool in 1997, by Stephen Lewis and Ken Heaton. This helps assess how long the stool has spent in the bowel, classifying the form of human faeces into seven categories. Type 1, constipation has spent the longest time in the bowel and type 7, diarrhoea the least time. A normal stool should be a type 3, (looks like a brown corn cob/sausage) or 4, (looks like a smooth sausage).

Music:

The interest in the effects of music on the brain has led to a new branch of research called neuromusicology which explores how the nervous system reacts to music. Research suggests listening to and playing music can make you smarter, happier, healthier and more productive at all stages of life.

A Sampling of Other Music with Lyrics and Beats that can Inspire:

- Don't Worry Be Happy - Bobby McFerrin
- Dare To Dream - John Farnham & Olivia Newton John
- The Greatest Love of All - Whitney Houston
- Love My Life - Robbie Williams

Mozart to Binaural beats; Solfeggio to Gandharva Veda music.

Binaural beats require a person to listen to different sound frequencies for a set amount of time, without any distractions, and in a comfortable space. Researchers believe these changes occur because the binaural beats activate specific systems within the brain.

Solfeggio frequencies make up the ancient 6-tone scale thought to have been used in sacred music.

Gandharva Veda is a Consciousness-Based Music Therapy. Maharishi Ayur-Veda Gandharva Veda music is a precious discipline of Maharishi's Vedic Science, the science of life, to create balance in nature, eliminate stress in the atmosphere, and produce a healthy influence for the individual and peace for the world family. As a part of the Veda, Gandharva Veda is the tradition of musical performance that replicates the vibrations of nature at different times of day and night.

Alignment:

I refer to this often within the book, alignment also includes spinal alignment, and you may utilise tools and practitioners such as craniosacral therapy or osteopathy. Chiropractic adjustments can be good too. Other forms of body work such as acupuncture and acupressure can be worth exploring as well.

Yoga gets mentioned quite a bit also. There are many forms of this, so once again align with what is right for you. I started out with Hatha yoga, yoga for health. Here are some of the yoga practices: Hatha yoga. Ashtanga yoga. Vinyasa yoga. Iyengar yoga. Yin yoga. Kundalini yoga. Bikram yoga. Power yoga.

I mention Qigong which is considered the grandfather of Tai chi. Pilates is another well-known practice that many enjoy and benefit from.

Taking a Measure:

I refer to "managing what you measure." This refers to your finances, your body and even your bloods. Knowing your numbers here is very handy too. Your vitamin D levels, the 'sunshine vitamin.' Be aware of the UV Index, what it measures as well, for best times in the sun. B12, especially if you are not eating meat. C-Reactive protein (CRP). High-sensitivity C-reactive protein (hs-CRP) and HbA1C Blood Glucose, are a few you may want to explore the next time you are having bloods done.

C-Reactive protein (CRP) increases when there is inflammation within your body. High-sensitivity C-reactive protein (hs-CRP) is often related to your Heart, cardiovascular disease risk.

The HbA1C is our 3-month blood sugar level.

Know the optimal numbers and work towards achieving and maintaining these. Be aware labs can have a different range for what's normal.

Blood glucose for example 2-5 is currently considered normal and 5-7 is pre diabetic.

Further Information Regarding Blood Markers to Test:

Andrew Huberman and Dr. Casey Means recommend a range of essential biomarkers for assessing overall health and specific conditions.

Dr. Casey Means' Recommended Blood Markers:

1. ApoB - Important for cardiovascular health
2. Uric Acid - Indicator of gout and kidney health
3. Fasting Insulin - Crucial for understanding metabolic functions
4. HOMA (Homeostatic Model Assessment) - Measuring insulin resistance
5. Iron Levels - Key for detecting anaemia and other conditions
6. hsCRP (high-sensitivity C-Reactive Protein) - Marker for inflammation
7. Liver Function Tests (GGT) - Assessing liver health

Andrew Huberman's Recommended Blood Markers:

1. IGF-1 (Insulin-like Growth Factor 1) - Linked to growth hormone levels
2. Testosterone - Important for both men and women
3. Estrogen - Present as oestradiol in tests, relevant for

both genders

4. Free Testosterone - Measures unbound testosterone
5. Dihydrotestosterone (DHT) - Important for androgenic activity
6. Cortisol - Should be checked in the morning, fasted
7. Creatinine - Monitors kidney function, consider creatine intake
8. LDL Cholesterol - Key cardiovascular risk factor
9. ApoB - Another cardiovascular marker
10. Sex Hormone Binding Globulin (SHBG) - Relevant for hormone transport
11. Progesterone and Prolactin - Especially important for women

For women, it's crucial to time these tests according to the menstrual cycle (mid-follicular or mid-luteal phase) for consistency. This helps accurately measure hormonal fluctuations and related health insights.

Another one I, (Robyn) like to get plenty of:

This is vitamin N. Vitamin N won't be on the bloods list as it is N for Nature. With this delightful one in mind, you will often see my husband and I hiking the hills wherever we are. Do wave and say hi if you see us.

GBOMBS: Acronym by Dr Joel Fuhrman. Twenty-Seven Research References:

Greens, cruciferous vegetables, like kale, spinach, broccoli:1-3

Beans and other legumes: 4-7

Onions and garlic: 8-11

Mushrooms:12-15

Berries:16-22

Seeds and nuts:23-27

1. Zhang X, Shu XO, Xiang YB, et al. **Cruciferous vegetable consumption is associated with a reduced risk of total and cardiovascular disease mortality.** Am J Clin Nutr 2011, **94**:240-246

2. Pollock RL. **The effect of green leafy and cruciferous vegetable intake on the incidence of cardiovascular disease: A meta-analysis.** JRSM Cardiovasc Dis 2016, **5**:2048004016661435.

3. Higdon J, Delage B, Williams D, Dashwood R. **Cruciferous vegetables and human cancer risk: epidemiologic evidence and mechanistic basis.** Pharmacol Res 2007, **55**:224-236.

4. Papanikolaou Y, Fulgoni VL, 3rd. **Bean consumption is associated with greater nutrient intake, reduced systolic blood pressure, lower body weight, and a smaller waist circumference in adults: results from the National Health and Nutrition Examination Survey 1999-2002.** J Am Coll Nutr 2008, **27**:569-576.

5. Jayalath VH, de Souza RJ, Sievenpiper JL, et al. **Effect of dietary pulses on blood pressure: a systematic review and meta-analysis of controlled feeding trials.** Am J Hypertens 2014, **27**:56-64.

6. Bazzano LA, Thompson AM, Tees MT, et al. **Non-soy legume consumption lowers cholesterol levels: a meta-analysis of randomized controlled trials.** Nutrition, metabolism, and cardiovascular diseases : NMCD 2011, **21**:94-103.

7. Sievenpiper JL, Kendall CW, Esfahani A, et al. **Effect of non-oil-seed pulses on glycaemic control: a systematic review and meta-analysis of randomised controlled experimental trials in people with and without diabetes.** Diab tologia 2009, **52**:1479-1495.

8. Rahman K, Lowe GM. **Garlic and cardiovascular disease: a critical review.** J Nutr 2006, **136**:736S-740S.

9. Powolny A, Singh S. **Multitargeted prevention and therapy of cancer by diallyl trisulfide and related**

Allium vegetable-derived organosulfur compounds. Cancer Lett 2008, **269**:305-314.

10. Bradley JM, Organ CL, Lefer DJ. **Garlic-Derived Organic Polysulfides and Myocardial Protection.** J Nutr 2016, **146**:403S-409S.

11. Galeone C, Pelucchi C, Levi F, et al. **Onion and garlic use and human cancer.** Am J Clin Nutr 2006, **84**:1027-1032.

12. Borchers AT, Krishnamurthy A, Keen CL, et al. **The Immunobiology of Mushrooms.** Exp Biol Med 2008, **233**:259-276.

13. Jeong SC, Koyyalamudi SR, Pang G. **Dietary intake of Agaricus bisporus white button mushroom accelerates salivary immunoglobulin A secretion in healthy volunteers.** Nutrition 2012, **28**:527-531.

14. Li J, Zou L, Chen W, et al. **Dietary mushroom intake may reduce the risk of breast cancer: evidence from a meta-analysis of observational studies.** PLoS One 2014, **9**:e93437.

15. Chen S, Oh SR, Phung S, et al. **Anti-aromatase activity of phytochemicals in white button mushrooms (Agaricus bisporus).** Cancer Res 2006, **66**:12026-12034.

16. Krikorian R, Shidler MD, Nash TA, et al. **Blueberry supplementation improves memory in older adults.** Journal of agricultural and food chemistry 2010, **58**:3996-4000.

17. Bowtell JL, Aboo-Bakkar Z, Conway M, et al. **Enhanced task related brain activation and resting perfusion in healthy older adults after chronic blueberry supplementation.** Appl Physiol Nutr Metab 2017.

18. Stoner GD, Wang LS, Casto BC. **Laboratory and clinical studies of cancer chemoprevention by antioxidants in berries.** Carcinogenesis 2008, **29**:1665-1674.

19. Cassidy A, Mukamal KJ, Liu L, et al. **High anthocyanin intake is associated with a reduced risk of myocardial**

infarction in young and middle-aged women. Circulation 2013, **127**:188-196.

20. Cassidy A, O'Reilly EJ, Kay C, et al. **Habitual intake of flavonoid subclasses and incident hypertension in adults.** Am J Clin Nutr 2011, **93**:338-347.

21. Johnson SA, Figueroa A, Navaei N, et al. **Daily blueberry consumption improves blood pressure and arterial stiffness in postmenopausal women with pre- and stage 1-hypertension: a randomized, double-blind, placebo-controlled clinical trial.** J Acad Nutr Diet 2015, **115**:369-377.

22. Whyte AR, Schafer G, Williams CM. **Cognitive effects following acute wild blueberry supplementation in 7- to 10-year-old children.** Eur J Nutr 2016, **55**:2151-2162.

23. Mattes RD, Dreher ML. **Nuts and healthy body weight maintenance mechanisms.** Asia Pac J Clin Nutr 2010, **19**:137-141.

24. Grosso G, Yang J, Marventano S, et al. **Nut consumption on all-cause, cardiovascular, and cancer mortality risk: a systematic review and meta-analysis of epidemiologic studies.** Am J Clin Nutr 2015, **101**:783-793.

25. Kris-Etherton PM, Hu FB, Ros E, Sabate J. **The role of tree nuts and peanuts in the prevention of coronary heart disease: multiple potential mechanisms.** *J Nutr* 2008, **138**:1746S-1751S.

26. Buck K, Zaineddin AK, Vrieling A, et al. **Meta-analyses of lignans and enterolignans in relation to breast cancer risk.** *Am J Clin Nutr* 2010, **92**:141-153.

27. Thompson LU, Chen JM, Li T, et al. **Dietary flaxseed alters tumor biological markers in postmenopausal breast cancer.** *Clin Cancer Res* 2005, **11**:3828-3835.

There are numerous online sources - Podcasts, YouTube, Documentaries and Summits available for you to explore too.

Be discerning.

- Be a lifelong learner and appreciator of life.
- Link into more of your own loving kindness, power and wisdom.
- Connect with others.
- Connect with nature.

"Peace begins with me."

A FINAL TALE TO CONCLUDE

The Tale of the Two Wolves. A Cherokee Indian Legend.

The Cherokee are known for their rich culture, history, and traditions. They have a rich tradition of storytelling, art, spirituality, and food. They also have a strong connection to the land and a commitment to stewardship. They value group harmony, integrity, honesty, perseverance, courage, respect, trust, honour, and humility.

An old Cherokee Indian is teaching his grandson about life, and says:

"A terrible fight is going on inside me between two wolves."

"One is evil - he is anger, envy, sorrow, regret, greed, arrogance, self-pity, guilt, resentment, inferiority, lies, false pride, superiority and ego."

"The other is good - he is joy, peace, love, hope, serenity, humility, kindness, benevolence, empathy, generosity, truth, compassion and faith."

"The same fight is going on inside you and inside every other person too."

The grandson thought about this for a while, then asked his grandfather: "Which wolf will win?"

His grandfather replied: "The one you feed."

Feed your soul and enjoy your keys to freedom.

You can also connect with me through:
Website https://robynhodgecoaching.com
Facebook https://facebook.com/robynhodgecoaching
Instagram https://www.instagram.com/hodgerobyn

ABOUT THE AUTHOR

My Story

Welcome, my name is Robyn Hodge. At the age of 16 when I thought the world was my oyster and I could do anything, I blacked out and sunk to the bottom of a swimming pool. One moment I was training for a triathlon and the next I was in a hospital bed finding out that I had almost died.

From this came a sea of challenges to face. I wanted to find other ways, ones that felt better, higher and free. I decided no one could change me but me. I could either live a life of challenges and fear or use my fear as fuel and turn my life around.

And so I did.

For every situation that would arise, instead of running or resenting it I faced it and even leaned into it. I chose to see it as a gift rather than a heavy burden life had for me. I decided to use it to learn, get stronger, wiser. I didn't want to go with that flow and drown anymore. To others it appeared my outlook was "Polly Anna" that I was sticking my head in the sand rather than being in the "real world." But it was the complete opposite. I had made a conscious choice that my freedom was my responsibility, and I will create "my world" and live it in my highest best way.

Using habits that would change my mind, body and spirit my life experiences shifted. Doing this regardless of what stage and age I am at.

I delve into that which relates to personal and professional development for the highest good of all regardless of background, country or experience. I love working with and seeing people from all over the globe light up even more. I have travelled extensively, researching and experiencing many cultures and ways of living to find the best ways forward.

The keys to freedom in your life may be different to others, reach out, connect and ignite more of yours.

I grew up on a farm in a remote part of Southland, New Zealand. I now live in the garden city of Christchurch. Some of my best teachers and inspiration for following my passions and being the next best version of myself are my husband and two children. I am also very grateful for all the wonderful family, friends and people who are, and have been a part of my life too.

Travel

My love of travel was a burning desire from a young age. I was keen to see how the rest of the world lived, and what made people tick. This 'people tick', meant understanding other cultures and countries, their beliefs and ways of living. What are the things that make people behave in the ways they do? How can we bring out the best in ourselves and one another? My travels have covered over 70 countries and 6 continents so far.

Career

I've been an employee, a business owner, a volunteer, a business coach, a manager, a fitness instructor, a counsellor for youth, a cancer prevention local director, working in Financial Services, Hospitality, Logistics, Mining, Health and Wellness Industries. I am a wife, a mother and a friend too.

Studies

Communication, Psychology, Leadership, Business, Financial Services, High Performance. I was part of the High-Performance Academy and also completed the Total Product Blueprint.

Quantum Physics, Neuroscience, Philosophy, Ayurvedic Medicine. I did undergraduate studies with the BPI Physic Institute as well.

The Healing Arts, Yoga, Qigong, Spirituality, Astrology, EFT - Emotional Freedom Technique, Numerology.

Certificates in Personal Health and Fitness, Consciousness, Body, Physiology and the Environment - Vedic Agriculture, Energy Healing. Coaching Weight Loss, Diet and Nutrition Coaching, Holistic Cancer Coaching and Cancer Prevention, Ho'oponopono Practitioner, Tutoring English as a Second Language.

Diplomas in Human Resources, Human Nutrition, Business Management and Entrepreneurship.

Meditator of Transcendental Meditation.

Exploring, Volunteering, Supporting

I could be hiking the hills, taking photos, going on other adventures or doing volunteer work with and for: Food Rescue, Food Bank. Bellyful, Delivering Free meals to families with babies or young children who need support. Tutoring English to Refugees and Migrants.

Supporting people on their journey and seeing them light up and into another level of their brilliance, that's simply awesome to be a part of too.

Keys to Freedom Series

I wrote and published this book: *Keys to Freedom. How to unlock your ability to thrive in changing times* and co-created the *Keys to Freedom Journal* along with the *Motivation, Inspiration and Gratitude* quote card sets. They are all infused with love to support and assist no matter where on this journey we may be.

Holistic Coaching

I'm humbled to work with you. Thanks so much for connecting in and choosing to step into more of your brilliances also. My coaching practice, Robyn Hodge Coaching. Holistic Coaching. Elevate Your Business, Enhance Your Wellbeing, Prosper Together. To see my offerings and to book in a chat: https://calendly.com/robynhodgecoaching/keys

"To anyone who wants to be heard from a deeper level and get results in their life."

"She is her own walking, talking advertisement for the effectiveness of her coaching systems and strategies."

THANKING THE READER

I hope that you have enjoyed reading and hearing this book so much. I always love it when people say they needed to read or hear that today and find the gems in here to serve them well. May this be part of your experience and you feel uplifted and inspired too. Keep referring to this book and notice how each time you do, you find more gems, reminders and even gentle nudges to enhance your life further.

It has been quite a journey and privilege to write and read out *Keys to Freedom. How to Unlock Your Ability to Thrive in Changing Times.* It is also an honour to be on this journey with you.

Whether we get to meet or not, my wish is that you enjoy an enlightening, blissful, vibrantly healthy life with great success in all your endeavours.

I would also greatly appreciate you taking five minutes to leave a short review on Amazon and Goodreads for this book and the audiobook as well. You'll find the audiobook on many platforms including Spotify. Your reviews make a beautiful difference to me and many. Thank you.

Goodreads:

https://www.goodreads.com/book/show/40652423-keys-to-freedom

Amazon: This can be done by clicking on the book link on your Amazon order.

Reviews are essential for visibility so that more readers can also benefit from this book.

I Am Eternally Grateful.

www.ingramcontent.com/pod-product-compliance
Lightning Source LLC
Chambersburg PA
CBHW071424090426
42737CB00011B/1562